"How To Build A Website With Wordpress...Fast!"

(3rd Edition)

By

Kent Mauresmo
Ana Pertrova

Copyright

Legal Terms

Disclaimer & Terms Of Use

The information contained in this material (including, but not limited to any manuals, CDs, recordings, MP3s or other content in any format) is based on sources and information reasonably believed to be accurate as of the time it was recorded or created. However, this material deals with topics that are constantly changing and are subject to ongoing changes RELATED TO TECHNOLOGY AND THE MARKETPLACE AS WELL AS LEGAL AND RELATED COMPLIANCE ISSUES. Therefore, the completeness and current accuracy of the materials cannot be guaranteed. These materials do not constitute legal, compliance, financial, tax, accounting, or related advice.

The end user of this information should therefore use the contents of this program and the materials as a general guideline and not as the ultimate source of current information and when appropriate the user should consult their own legal, accounting or other advisors.

Any case studies, examples, illustrations are not intended to guarantee, or to imply that the user will achieve similar results. In fact, your results may vary significantly and factors such as your market, personal effort and many other circumstances may and will cause results to vary.

THE INFORMATION PROVIDED IN THIS PRODUCT IS SOLD AND PROVIDED ON AN „AS IS" BASIS WITHOUT ANY EXPRESS OR IMPLIED WARRANTIES, OF ANY KIND WHETHER WARRANTIES FOR A PARTICULAR PURPOSE OR OTHER WARRANTY except as may be specifically set forth in the materials or in the site. IN PARTICULAR, THE SELLER OF THE PRODUCT AND MATERIALS DOES NOT WARRANT THAT ANY OF THE INFORMATION WILL PRODUCE A PARTICULAR ECONOMIC RESULT OR THAT IT WILL BE SUCCESSFUL IN CREATING PARTICULAR MARKETING OR SALES RESULTS. THOSE RESULTS ARE YOUR RESPONSIBILITY AS THE END USER OF THE PRODUCT. IN PARTICULAR, SELLER SHALL NOT BE LIABLE TO USER OR ANY OTHER PARTY FOR ANY DAMAGES, OR COSTS, OF ANY CHARACTER INCLUDING BUT NOT LIMITED TO DIRECT OR INDIRECT, CONSEQUENTIAL, SPECIAL, INCIDENTAL, OR OTHER COSTS OR DAMAGES, IN EXCESS OF THE PURCHASE PRICE OF THE PRODUCT OR SERVICES. THESE LIMITATIONS MAY BE AFFECTED BY THE LAWS OF PARTICULAR STATES AND JURISDICTIONS AND AS SUCH MAY BE APPLIED IN A DIFFERENT MANNER TO A PARTICULAR USER.

Contents

QUICK INTRODUCTION 1

CHAPTER 1. 2

    WORDPRESS.COM VS. WORDPRESS.ORG 2

    WHAT'S YOUR NICHE? 3

    PICK A TARGETED DOMAIN NAME 4

    PURCHASING A DOMAIN NAME & WEB HOSTING 4

    HOW TO SET-UP A WORDPRESS WEBSITE USING BLUEHOST 5

    OTHER HOSTING OPTIONS 15

    WEB HOSTING GUIDE 16

    YOUR WEBSITE IS LIVE! 16

    LOG INTO YOUR WEBSITE 17

    DO YOU NEED TECH SUPPORT AT 2AM? 18

CHAPTER 2. 19

    WORDPRESS PLUGINS 19

    BONUS TIP 23

CHAPTER 3. 27

    WORDPRESS THEMES 27

    MORE THEME OPTIONS 32

CHAPTER 4. 33

    WORDPRESS PAGES AND MENUS 33

    LINK TO HOMEPAGE 34

    THEME OPTIONS 39

CHAPTER 5 42

    CUSTOM SIDEBAR 42

    EDIT YOUR WIDGETS THE EASY WAY 43

    FOOTERS & HTML CODE 44

CHAPTER 6. 46

    USER SETTINGS 46

    ADD NEW USER 46

PERSONAL OPTIONS   47

CONTACT INFO   48

ABOUT YOURSELF   49

CHAPTER 7.   52

SETTINGS   52

GENERAL SETTINGS   52

WRITING SETTINGS   53

READING SETTINGS   53

DISCUSSION SETTINGS   55

MEDIA SETTINGS   55

PERMALINK SETTINGS   56

WORDPRESS PLUGIN SETTINGS   56

CHAPTER 8   57

PLUGIN SETTINGS   57

META TAGS   57

ALL IN ONE SEO   59

GOOGLE XML SITEMAPS   60

RELATED POSTS THUMBNAILS   60

PAGENAVI SETTINGS   62

WORDPRESS BACKUP TO DROPBOX PLUGIN   63

SHAREAHOLIC PLUGIN (SEXY BOOKMARKS)   64

WP MAINTENANCE PLUGIN   66

HYPER CACHE   68

JETPACK PLUGIN   69

CHAPTER 9.   72

BLOG POST SETTINGS   72

BLOG POST TITLE   72

PERMALINK   73

ADD MEDIA FILES   74

TOOLBAR   75

TEXT   76

METADATA   78

ALL IN ONE SEO PACK 79

CATEGORIES, TAGS, FEATURED IMAGE 80

TAGS 82

FEATURED IMAGE 82

PREVIEW/PUBLISH 84

CHAPTER 10. 87

MORE DASHBOARD FEATURES: MEDIA TAB 87

COMMENTS TAB 88

WHEN SHOULD YOU USE THE "EDIT " COMMENT FEATURE? 88

HOW TO GET BLOG COMMENTS 89

TOOLS TAB 90

CHAPTER 11. 91

WHAT'S AN RSS FEED? 91

LEARN HOW RSS FEEDS WORK 91

HOW TO ADD AN RSS FEED TO YOUR WEBSITE 93

BONUS TIP 96

BONUS INFO 97

CHAPTER 12. 98

DO YOU WANT TO SELL PRODUCTS ONLINE? 98

EMAIL LIST 98

SQUEEZE PAGES AND SALES PAGES 99

SHOPPING CARTS 100

SELL PHYSICAL PRODUCTS 101

CREATE A MEMBERSHIP SITE 102

CREATE VIDEO'S FOR YOUR WEBSITE 103

CONCLUSION 106

PDF VERSION OF THIS EBOOK 107

MORE FROM THIS AUTHOR 108

Quick Introduction

My name is Kent Mauresmo and I'm one of the bloggers at www.Read2Learn.net. This is our 3rd WordPress guide written to help beginners like you create and manage your own WordPress website.

When I first started using WordPress, I had a very hard time trying to learn how to use WordPress effectively. I remember searching *Google* and *YouTube* for **hours** trying to figure out how to build a website with WordPress. Trust me; most of the free information on Google is completely useless and unnecessarily complicated.

A lot of people that'll *try* to teach you how to use WordPress barely know the basics themselves. It's the blind leading the blind, and you'll just end up wasting your valuable time and money.

How is this book different?

I actively use WordPress, and I'm learning something new about it every day. This book will teach you how to **easily** use WordPress to create simple **blogs**, **full blown websites**, **membership websites**, and **video marketing pages**.

Visit the links below to check out a few blogs and/or websites that I've created using WordPress:

- http://read2learn.net (simple blog)
- http://read2learn.biz (simple membership style website)
- http://TheShapingSpacesGroup.com (standard website)
- http://PCHstaging.com (flash style website)
- http://MyDormRoomWall.com (Photo Gallery)

If you'd like to learn how to **easily** create similar websites as the one's mentioned above, then **this is the book for you**. This step-by-step guide is fast paced and easy to follow.

Quick Disclaimer: I am not an accomplished *New York Times* bestselling author, so this book might have some flaws and maybe a few grammatical errors. If you read for style or for literary quality, then this probably isn't the book for you.

This book is designed to do one thing….SAVE YOU TIME!

If you're ready to **build your first website** (or blog) fast; then follow our step-by-step guide and we won't let you down. Let's get started!

Chapter 1.

WordPress.com vs. Wordpress.org

WordPress.com and WordPress.org are two different platforms. WordPress.com offers a 100% free service designed for blogs. WordPress.com is similar to *Live Journal* and *Blogger*.

If you sign up for free at WordPress.com, you'll get a free domain name like "read2learn.wordpress.com" which isn't very professional for business. Since the service is free, you'll also have very limited disk space and your website will be full of advertisements. Here are a few reasons why you shouldn't choose WordPress.com

WordPress.com

1. If you want to upgrade to a custom design, it will cost you **$30**.
2. Your free domain name will include the word "WordPress" as mentioned earlier (i.e. *read2learn.wordpress.com*.) To take the word "WordPress" out of your domain name, it will cost **$13/year**.
3. WordPress.com runs advertisements on your site. If you want the ads removed, it will cost **$30/year**.
4. Limited Space! If you need more space for pages and media, you'll have to pay for an upgrade for more space.
5. If you want to embed videos within your website or blog, you'll have to pay for an upgrade called "Video Press." Video Press cost **$60/year**.
6. If you want to transfer your blog from WordPress.com to WordPress.org, they have a "Guided Transfer Fee" of **$129**.
7. If you want to set up a redirect so your WordPress.com site forwards to a new website, it will cost **$13/year**.
8. You can't place any advertisements on your WordPress.com website.
9. You can't upload additional themes or plugins on your WordPress.com website.
10. Your blog/website is hosted at WordPress.com. Since they're hosting your site, they run the show! They can terminate your access to all or any part of the website at any time with or without cause, with or without notice, effective immediately.

WordPress.org

This is what you want! WordPress.org gives you a link to download the WordPress software. The software is free, but you need to have your own web hosting company to host the software for you.

You don't need to download the software from WordPress.org. Most web hosting providers already have the WordPress software ready to install for you.

Using the WordPress.org software will give you more flexibility and save you a lot of money. With the WordPress.org software, you only need to:

1. Pay $2-$13/year for a professional domain name with a hosting company like GoDaddy or Bluehost. Bluehost is actually preferred because they'll give you a free domain name and they're the #1 recommended by WordPress.org.
2. Pay $70-90/year for web hosting depending on the package you choose.
3. Have your hosting company install the <u>WordPress.org</u> software for free! (One-click installation.)
4. Create whatever type of website you want with unlimited space and bandwidth. Perfect!

As you can see, it makes more sense to create a website using the "WordPress.org" software. You'll have more control over your website/blog, and you won't have to pay for any unnecessary upgrades.

Some people have tried to use the information in our books to create a website using WordPress.com. If you're trying to create a free blog at WordPress.com, then this book might confuse you. This book is designed to teach you how to create and manage a professional websites using the **WordPress.org** software.

I hope you know the difference between WordPress.com and WordPress.org now. WordPress.com is a free blogging platform like Live Journal. It's 100% free to use, but it's not ideal for business owners.

WordPress.org gives you the software to create whatever type of website you want. This is the ideal choice if you want to create a website for business with little to no limitations.

The next step is to decide what your website is going to be about. You'll also need to perform some research before you choose a domain name.

What's Your Niche?

Decide what niche your website will be about, and then **narrow it down** to something more specific. For example, let's say you're good at "dog training" so you decide that you want to create a website teaching people how to train dogs.

Since "dog training" is a very competitive niche, it's better to go after a more specific niche like "Dog Training for Poodles." This tactic will put you 10 steps ahead of your competition because you're targeting a specific audience.

It's important to note that someone who wants to <u>purchase</u> a training course to train their poodle will most likely type into Google, "How to Train Poodles" instead of something generic like "Dog Training."

Pick a Targeted Domain Name

So let's assume that your niche will be "Dog Training for Poodles." Next you have to be creative and think of how people will search for information about "Poodle Training" in search engines.

For simplicity sake, let's just say that someone who's looking to train their Poodle will type into Google **"How to Train Poodles."** Perfect! Let's see if we can find a domain name that matches that exact phrase. (HowToTrainPoodles.com)

TIP: The closer your domain name matches a keyword phrase typed into Google, the better chance your website will have showing up in the top ten Google search results.

Purchasing a Domain Name & Web Hosting

There are multiple places to buy domain names and web hosting for WordPress. Most web hosting providers will have more than enough resources to host a WordPress website because WordPress is very simple software.

The Top 3 Hosting Providers I Recommend For WordPress Are:

1. Bluehost
2. GoDaddy
3. InMotion

There are thousands of web hosting companies, so feel free to do your own research. The average reliable web hosting plan will cost you anywhere from $5-$15/month.

Most hosting providers will give you the option to prepay your hosting account for 12, 24, or 36 months. The longer you prepay your account for, the bigger discount you'll receive.

The web hosts I've recommended offer:

- The best customer service
- Reliable fast hosting
- Specialize in WordPress web hosting
- Excellent tech support
- One-click install for WordPress
- Money back guarantee

If you're on a really tight budget, then GoDaddy offers month-to-month web hosting plans which will save you some money up-front.

Check out our recommended web hosting providers to see if they're within your budget. If you search Google and Bing for the "**best WordPress hosting 2014**" you'll notice the same companies I've just mentioned.

If you decide to choose a different company, make sure that you do as much research on the company as possible. It's a huge headache to move your website from one host to another, and it's take a lot of time. So make sure that you choose a reliable web host the first time.

Important Disclaimer

Since there are thousands of web hosts; it's impossible for me to show you step-by-step how to install WordPress for <u>every single</u> hosting provider. In the next section, I'll show you how to purchase a domain name, web hosting, and install the WordPress software using Bluehost.

The reason I'm going to use Bluehost for this example is because WordPress.org officially recommends this hosting provider. Bluehost will also give you a **FREE** domain name for the first year which will save you an extra $15.

If you decide to use another hosting provider; they'll also have a step-by-step guide on their website showing you how to install WordPress which will very look similar to what you're about to see. If you get stuck trying to install WordPress, do not panic!

Just purchase your domain name and your hosting package. After you've made your purchase, **<u>contact customer support over the phone</u>** (call over the phone for optimal support) and ask tech support to show you how to install WordPress on your domain name.

Tech support will walk you through the process in less than 10 minutes. That's what they're getting paid for, so put them to good use. They'll be excited to help you install WordPress on your new hosting account!

The following example with Bluehost is just to show you how easy the process is. If you're comfortable with computers, then feel free to install WordPress yourself using the "one-click install" feature.

How to Set-Up a WordPress Website Using Bluehost

To check the availability of a domain name, you have to go to the "Bluehost sign-up page." For this example, I'm going to search to see if <u>HowToTrainPoodles.com</u> is available.

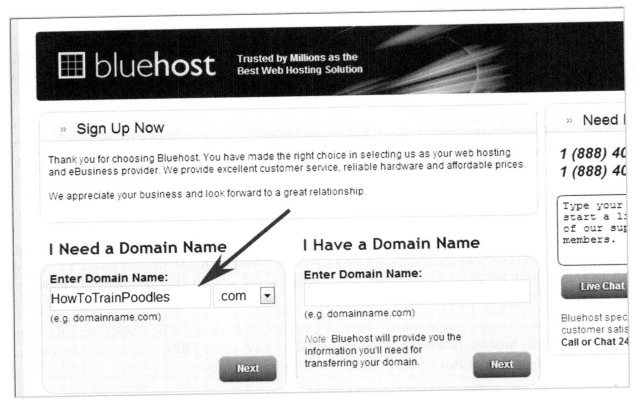

Enter the domain name you're interested in into Bluehost's sign-up page and click the "**NEXT**" button to see if the domain name is available or not! If the domain name you want is unavailable, you'll see a screen that'll give you alternate suggestions. If you don't like the alternative suggestions, then you can manually search for a different domain.

If the domain you want is available, then you'll see a screen that says "**Congratulations!**" Now Bluehost will prompt you to enter your <u>name</u>, <u>address</u>, <u>phone number</u>, and <u>email address</u> so you can claim your *Free* domain name.

Next, you'll see the "*Package Information*" section. This is where **you need to pick your hosting account plan** because you need to host your website. There are only 5 options here, so I'll just tell you what to do to save you some time:

- **Account Plan** – Select the "12 Month Price" option from the drop down list.
- **SiteLock Domain Security** – No! Uncheck that box because you don't need it.
- **Site Backup Pro** – No! Uncheck that box because you don't need it.
- **Search Engine Jump Start** – No! Uncheck that box because you don't need it.
- **Domain Whois Privacy** – Yes, you should purchase this! When you register a website, all your information is public in the *Whois Database* including your address, phone number, and email. If you purchase the *Domain Whois Privacy*, then all your information is hidden from scammers and spammers. This feature will cost $9.99/year.

Package Information

Account Plan	12 Month Price - $6.95/mo. ▼
Setup Fee	**FREE**
Primary Domain Registration	**FREE**
SiteLock Domain Security	☐ - $14.99 per year <u>More information</u>
Site Backup Pro	☐ - $12.95 per year <u>More information</u>
Search Engine Jumpstart	☐ - $14.99 per year <u>More information</u>
Domain Whois Privacy	☑ - $9.99 per year **HIGHLY RECOMMENDED** <u>More information</u>

Billing Information

Card Type	Visa ▼

Now <u>enter your billing information</u>. Confirm that you have read and agree with Bluehost's terms of service, and then click on the "Next" button. The system will now verify your credit card information.

Keep in mind that you're investing in 12 months worth of hosting **up front**. So you're actually investing $6.95 x 12 which is $83.40. If you decide to go with the *Domain Whois Privacy*, then add $9.99 to that and your total investment is around $94. So just make sure that you use a credit/debit card that has at least $100 on it and you're <u>done for the year!</u>

After you hit the "Next" button, you'll be taken to another "Congratulations" page. On this page you need to set up a password to log into your Bluehost account. Click the link that says "**Create Your Password**."

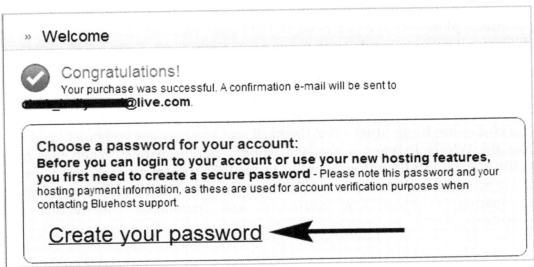

After you click that link, you'll be taken to a page that will prompt you to enter in a new password. Your **password must include**:

- At least 1 uppercase letter
- At least 1 number
- At least 1 symbol
- At least 1 lowercase letter
- At least 8 total characters

Here's an example of an acceptable password: **K3ntM@uresm0**

Below the password section, you'll need to enter a verification pin. The pin number you create is only used for verification purposes during interactions with **customer support**.

Your pin has to be 6-10 digits long, so just **use your phone number** because it's easy to remember. If you're not comfortable using a phone number, then just use a random number and **email it to yourself** along with your new password. When you're finish, click the submit button.

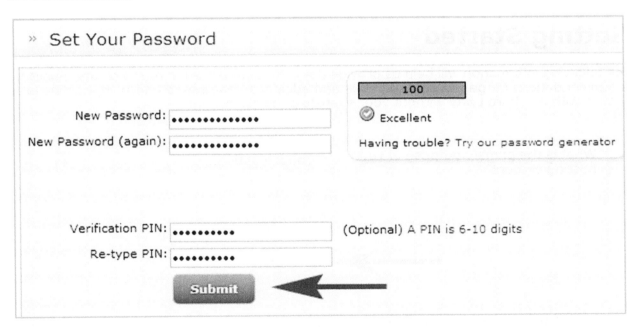

After you click the "submit" button, your password will update and Bluehost will automatically log you out the system. Next you'll be prompted to **log back into Bluehost with your new password**. Enter in your new password and click the "Login" button.

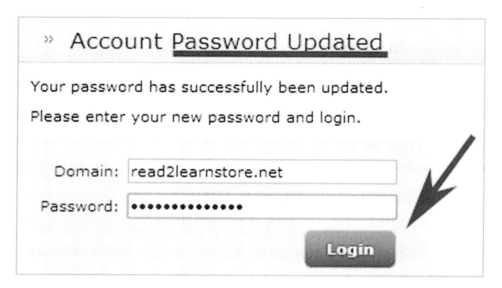

After you click the login button, you'll arrive at a "Getting Started" survey page. I know you're excited to get your website up and running, so you can click the "*No Thanks*" option to move on to the next page.

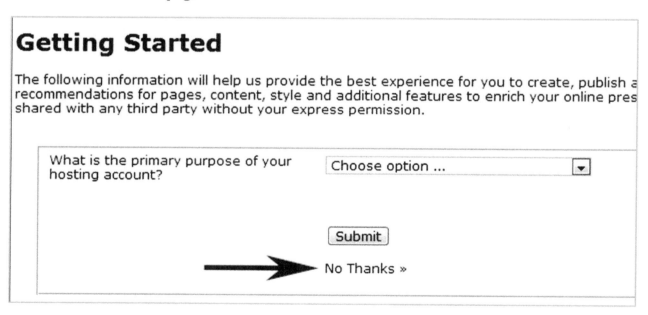

After you click "*No Thanks*", Bluehost will log you into your control panel A.K.A *cPanel*. This page will look overwhelming at first glance, but **this is the easiest part**!

Scroll down to about the <u>middle of the page</u>, and you'll see a section that says "**Site Builders**." Within that section, you'll see a WordPress logo. **Click on that logo**!

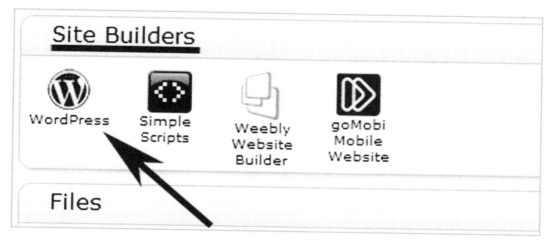

The next page that you'll arrive on is the WordPress installation page. You'll see a green button that says "**Start**" and that's what you need to click.

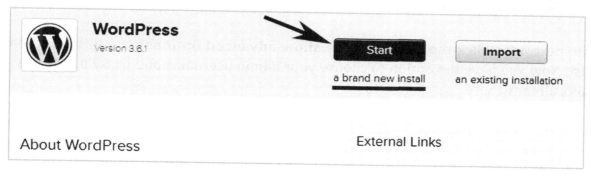

On the next page you'll need to select the domain name that you want to install WordPress on. After you choose your domain name, click the button that says "**Check Domain**."

On the next screen you'll get an error message that says, "*OOPS! Looks like something already exists there. I understand that continuing will overwrite the files.*" Select the check ox that says, "I understand that continuing will overwrite files."

Important: If you were running this installation on a website that you already have up and running, then you shouldn't overwrite the files. This isn't an issue here because it's a new website. Click "Check Domain" again.

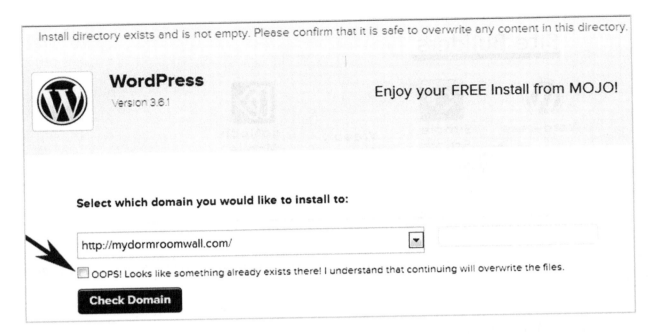

On the next page, click the box that says "**Show advanced options**" and this will expand the list. Now you have the option to choose your admin username and password or use the defaults already there.

This username and password will be used to log into the back-end of your WordPress website. This information will be emailed to you, but you might want to write it down too. Check the "terms and conditions" box, and then click the "Install Now" button.

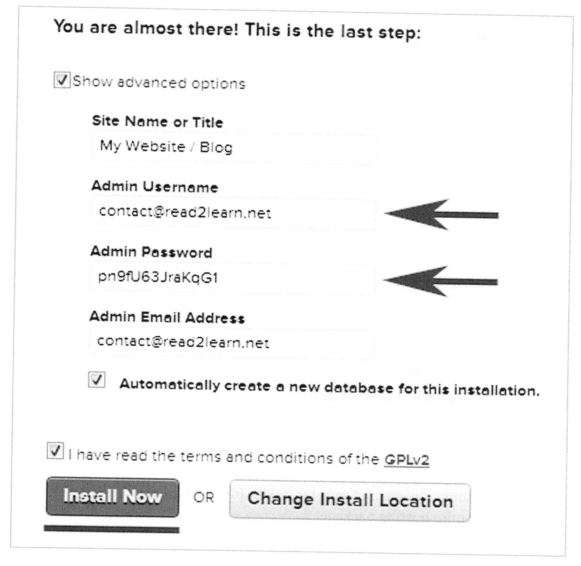

After you click the "Install Now" button, Bluehost will start to install WordPress on your domain name. It may take up to two minutes and then you're finally done!

Bluehost will display your **Site URL**, **Login URL**, **Username** and **Password** to access your new website! They'll also email this information to you, so make sure that you save that email into a designated folder or print it out.

Install Processes

Installation complete! You can access your new website using the following information.

INSTALL: http://mydormroomwall.com/
⚫ **Status:** success

STEP 1: Access your new install of WordPress

Site URL: http://mydormroomwall.com/

Login URL: http://mydormroomwall.com/wp-admin

Username: █████████████

Password: ███████████████

That pretty much covers everything! So in summary, here's what you'll need to do step by step:

1. Decide on a domain name and register it with Bluehost for free.
2. Pick the 12 month hosting package.
3. Grab your credit card and make the purchase.
4. Update your password with Bluehost.
5. Log back in with your new password, click the WordPress Logo within your control panel, and then click the "Start" button to begin the installation process.
6. Click on the "Advanced" option to set up a customized username and password to log into your website. DONE!

You can literally do all of these steps in about 10 minutes. I just explained everything in great detail to avoid confusion. If you're still confused, contact Bluehost's customer service over the phone, and they'll help you out right away.

Other Hosting Options

I realize that some of you don't want to use Bluehost to host your website. Some of you might prefer *GoDaddy, InMotion, Hostgator, etc.*

Very Important: Most other hosting companies will have 3 hosting packages. Never pick the cheapest hosting package! The cheapest hosting package will usually limit you to only <u>one website</u> for that plan.

You should at least choose the middle package which will allow you to add multiple websites to one hosting account. Look below at the hosting packages available through Go Daddy. The "Deluxe" and "Ultimate" hosting plans will allow you to build unlimited websites on a single hosting account.

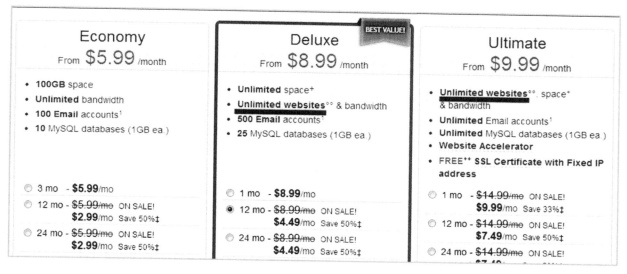

Bluehost only has one hosting package that offers unlimited everything. That's another reason why I recommend Bluehost because it's simple and cost effective for beginners.

Very Important: If you decide to choose another web host and you're having problems installing WordPress, just <u>contact the web host</u> over the phone. They'll help you install WordPress and your website will go live within an hour.

Installing WordPress on your hosting account is easier than ever before, and it should take less than 10 minutes. Do not allow yourself to get stuck or frustrated while trying to install WordPress. Just call customer support and ask for help!

When I created my first two websites, I personally called my hosting provider and asked customer support to walk me through the installation process. I wrote down all the steps, and I was eventually comfortable installing WordPress on my own.

Web Hosting Guide

<u>Limited Offer</u>: If you need additional help navigating through your web hosting account, then we've got you covered. For a limited time you can download our PDF book, "*WordPress Web Hosting: How to Use cPanel and Your Hosting Control Center.*"

Below is the link where you can download the book for **free**. Please don't share this link or we'll have to remove the free download:

- http://bestwebhostinginc.com/get-it-here

If you've already successfully installed WordPress and you're comfortable using your hosting account, then congratulations! You're ready to move on to the next step!

Your Website is Live!

Your website will go LIVE almost immediately after Bluehost says that your installation is complete. When your website goes live, it'll have the default (*not so attractive*) Wordpress theme.

This obviously doesn't look like a professional website, but we're just getting started. I'll show you how to easily change this theme into a beautiful website in the following chapters!

Log Into Your Website

You can log into the administration area of your website two different ways:

1.) There will be a link that says "**Log In**" on the sidebar of your homepage. Click that link and then enter the admin username and password that you set up with your web host.

2.) Type your domain name in the address bar, add "**/wp-admin**" at the end of your domain name, and then press the "enter" key on your keyboard!

After you click "Log In" or use the "/wp-admin" method, you'll be taken to a Wordpress screen that requires you to enter the username and password that you set up with your web host.

Once you're in the administration area of your website, you can change your settings, customize your website, and start creating content!

Do You Need Tech Support at 2am?

The recommended web hosts (*Bluehost, Go Daddy and Inmotion*) offer amazing customer support that's available 24/7/365. If you have questions or you're receiving error messages, just call them and put them to work! That's what you're paying them for.

Do you see how easy this is? Guess what? That was the hardest part! This is the exact reason why there are teenagers building websites and selling products and services online. Why would you pay a company $500 for something you can do yourself in couple of minutes?

In the next chapter, I'll show you how to <u>effectively</u> set up your website/blog within the administration area. It's very easy if you follow my lead.

Chapter 2.

WordPress Plugins

WordPress plugins are add-ons for your website. In this chapter I'll list several plugins that will help your website function better. To install plugins, you need to log into the administration area of your website. Once you're in your dashboard, you'll see the words "**Plugins**" and that's where you need to click.

After you click the plugins tab, the list will expand and you'll see the words "Add New." Click the words "Add New."

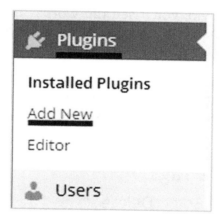

After you click "Add New", you'll be taken to a page where you can search for plugins that you'd like to install.

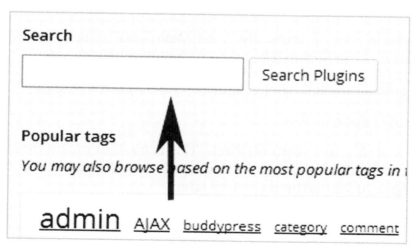

Now you need to search for plugins and install them into your blog. This is very simple and I'll show you how to install the best plugins in less than 5 minutes.

The first plugin I want you search for is:

1. **Add Meta Tags**

Name	Version	Rating
Add Meta Tags Details | Installed	2.4.1	★★★★½

The "Add Meta Tags" plugin helps search engines like Google, Yahoo, and Bing find your website. After you find this plugin, you'll see the words "**install now**" under the plugin. Click the "install now" link to install the plugin. If you want more details about the plugin, then click the "Details" link first to read more about a specific plugin.

After the plugin is installed, make sure that you click the "activate" link to activate the plugin. Alternatively you can also click the "Plugins" tab on the left column again. Now you'll see the "Add Meta Tags" plugin you just installed on your list of plugins.

Just click the "Activate" button under the "Add Meta Tags" plugin and now the plugin is active. Congratulations! You just installed your first plugin!

Repeat this same step for the following plugins:

2. **All in One SEO Pack**

S.E.O. stands for "Search Engine Optimization." This is another plugin that will help search engines find your website/blog so it'll be displayed in their search results. I'll show you how to set up this plugin for maximum benefit later.

3. Force Gzip

This plugin will help speed up your website.

4. Google XML Sitemaps

This plugin will help search engines like Google find all your blog posts and pages.

5. Hyper Cache

Hyper Cache is a cache system for WordPress to help improve its performance and save resources. You'll have to change a line of code for this plugin to work properly. I have a video on my blog showing you how it's done here: http://read2learn.net/hyper-cache

6. Related Post Thumbnails

At the end of each blog post, this plugin will show an image and a link that redirects readers to related blog posts on your website. This is an amazing plugin that will keep people on your website longer.

7. Shareaholic

This plugin will allow other people to share your blog posts on Facebook, Twitter, and other popular websites.

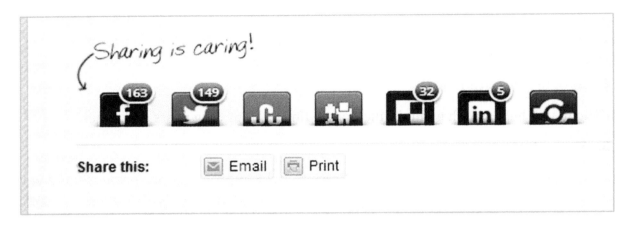

8. WP-PageNavi

This plugin will add a numbered page navigation toolbar to the bottom of your website.

9. Anti-Captcha

Help eliminate spam comments. This is an excellent alternative to the default "*Akismet*" plugin. I don't use Akismet.

10. WordPress Backup To Dropbox

Use this plugin to backup your website! It's very easy to use, and it only requires that you set up a free account at Dropbox. If you already have a Dropbox account, then you can use your existing account.

11. WP Maintenance Mode

This is an optional plugin that you can install. This plugin adds a "Maintenance Page" to your website that will let visitors know that your website is down for maintenance. This is a useful plugin if you're transferring your old website over to WordPress. You probably don't want your website "live" if you need to make major changes to your homepage.

12. Jetpack by WordPress.com (default plugin already installed)

This plugin has a few nice features. You can see a screenshot of what Jetpack by Wordpress looks like within your dashboard below. You'll notice plenty of options available to you through the Jetpack plugin.

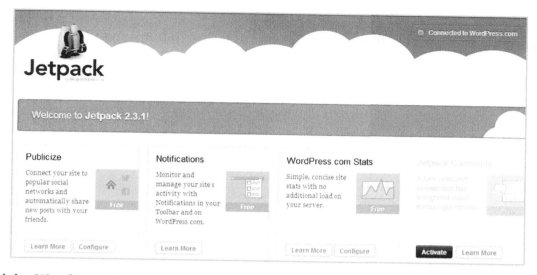

"Jetpack by WordPress" is already installed by default. This plugin has a unique feature that allows you to track your website visitors and stats. (Similar to Google Analytics.)

To activate the Jetpack plugin, you need to go to www.wordpress.com and create a free account. After you create an account at Wordpress.com, you'll be able to active this plugin with one click!

I'll show you how to set-up and customize all these plugins in another chapter. Just install them for now and we'll talk more about them later!

Bonus Tip

Set up a Gravatar

A gravatar is a picture image that shows up next to your blog comments. You can set up a gravatar by going to www.gravatar.com.

You can link one or multiple email addresses to your gravatar image. Every time you **leave a comment** on another WordPress website, there is a section for you to enter your email address. Just enter the email address that you set up at *www.gravatar.com*, and your picture image will show up on any blog that allows gravatar images.

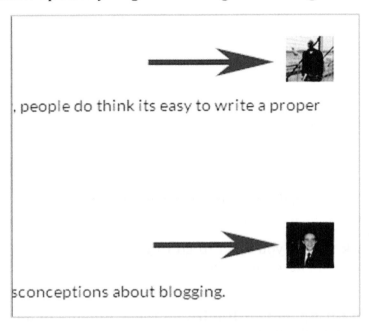

You can change the gravatar settings on your blog by clicking the "**Settings**" tab on your WordPress dashboard. Click the "discussion" link to open up the discussion options.

Now scroll down and you'll see that you have the option to show Avatars (Gravatar) or not show Avatars. You'll also have the option to set up a default Avatar for people that leave comments on your blog that don't have an Avatar.

Set this up however you like, and click the "Save Changes" button at the bottom of the page.

Set Up Permalinks

Under the **"Setting"** tab select "Permalinks." The default setting for your permalinks isn't search engine friendly, so select the "Post name" option instead.

This will create easy-to-read links that are easy for search engines to understand. For example, instead of website links that look like this:

http://read2learn.net/?p=123 (confusing to search engines)

The "post name" permalink structure will change your blog links look like this:

http://read2learn.net/how-to-blog (search engine friendly)

We're making good progress! Before I go into the next chapter, I'd like to direct your attention to the top right corner of your WordPress dashboard. You should see your **Username**, and below that you'll see something that says **"Screen Options"** and **"Help."**

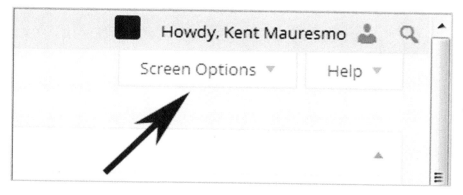

If you scroll your mouse over your username, you'll have the option to <u>log out</u> of your dashboard if you need to take a break! The **"Screen Options"** tab will give you different options depending on which screen you're on. (i.e. How many plugins, blog posts, or pages, to show on your screen.) The "**Help**" tab will provide with you additional resources if you'd like more information about a specific screen that you're on.

Okay, now it's time to upgrade your WordPress theme! In the next chapter I'll show you where to purchase a professional theme. I'll also show you how to easily install your new theme in less than 2 minutes.

Chapter 3.

WordPress Themes

The default theme for WordPress is okay, but I suggest that you upgrade if you want to be taken serious. You can Google "WordPress Themes" if you want to find your own sources, but I recommend using Theme Forest. The website is www.themeforest.net.

Theme Forest is **very easy** to navigate, and they have a special section dedicated to WordPress themes. The average theme will cost around $35, and it's very easy to install and customize these themes on your new website.

Follow the step-by-step instructions below to find and install a premium WordPress theme.

Step 1.

Go to www.themeforest.net and click "*Create Account*" at the top of the page. You have to create an account to purchase themes on this website.

You have to pick a username, password, enter your email address, first name, and last name. Next, go to your email inbox and verify your email address to complete your registration.

Step 2.

Go back to Theme Forest and make sure you're logged in. Now click the tab that says "Wordpress" at the top of the website. This will allow you to see a list of themes that are compatible with WordPress.

You can hover your mouse over each theme, and a pop-up window will display a preview of the theme. If you like what you see then click on the theme. You'll also see a list of categories on the right side of the screen if you want to refine your search.

After you click on a theme, you'll have the option to see screenshots or a live preview of the theme. I suggest that you click "**Live Preview**" to see exactly how a particular theme will look on your website.

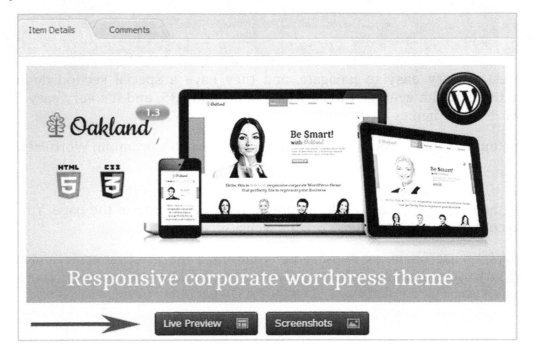

Here's a screenshot of a potential theme called "Oakland" that you can install on WordPress. This theme actually looks really nice, so I might buy this one myself!

After you find a theme that you like, click the purchase button on the top right hand corner. You'll be taken to a screen that'll ask you if you want to buy with "Prepaid Credit" or "Buy Now."

Click the **"Buy Now"** button. Theme Forest will charge you $2 extra for using this option, but that's better than using the prepaid option.

The prepaid option will require you to make a deposit of $10, $20, $30, $40, $50, etc. So if you're buying a theme that cost $35, it doesn't make sense to prepay your account $40.

After you click "Buy Now", you'll be taken to a PayPal screen where you'll need to enter your payment information. After you complete the payment, you'll be able to download the theme in a **zip file**. A zip file basically contains one or more files or folders that have been compressed. Make sure that you save the zip file to your desktop so it's easy to find it.

Step 3.

Log into your WordPress website and click the **"Appearance"** tab under your dashboard options. Make sure the "Themes" option is selected as well.

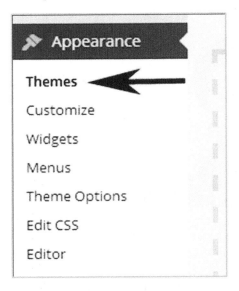

At the top of the page, you'll see a button that says "**Add New**" and that's where you need to click. After you click that link, you'll be taken to a page that'll give you the option to upload a new theme.

Click the "Upload" link and you'll be taken to a new page that will ask you to browse (or look for) the theme on your computer. (zip file only)

Now if you saved your new theme to your desktop, it'll be easy to find. So click "browse" to find your theme, and then double click on your themes zip file.

This will place the contents of your theme into the "browse" box on WordPress. The next step is to click the "install now" button and your theme will start to install on website.

IMPORTANT TIP: Some themes are packaged different. Sometimes the zip file provided to you from *Themeforest* is the actual theme. Other times, the actual theme might be within **another folder** inside that zip file.

Some of the really complicated themes will come with PDF documentation showing how to use the theme. Sometimes a theme will also include the <u>demo</u> content that was displayed when you clicked the "live preview" option on *Themeforest*. So make sure that you **examine the zip file** first to make sure you're uploading the right zip file!

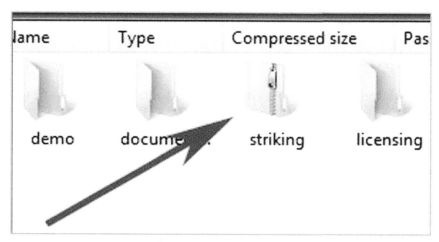

After you click the "upload" button to upload your theme, it shouldn't take longer than two minutes for your theme to install. You should see your new theme within the available themes area.

To activate the theme, just click the link that says "**Activate**" under the theme and you're done. You can repeat this process in the future if you decide to purchase another theme.

More Theme Options

If you don't like the themes available on *ThemeForest*, then you can try out these websites too:

- www.mojomarketplace.com
- www.woothemes.com
- www.elegantthemes.com

If you're on a really tight budget, then you can look for **free themes** by visiting www.WordPress.org. Click the "Themes" option on the top menu and you'll be presented with a list of free WordPress themes that you can download.

In the next chapter, I'll show you how to customize your new theme and add new pages to your website. It's really simple and only takes a couple minutes!

Chapter 4.

WordPress Pages and Menus

Hopefully you have your premium WordPress theme installed by now. If you decided to stick with the default WordPress theme, you can still follow the steps below to customize your pages.

You'll want to create a "**Home**" page, "**About Us**" page, and a "**Contact**" page. These are standard pages that all professional websites have.

If you're going to sell products, then you might also want to create a "**Products**" page, "**Privacy Policy**" page, and "**Terms & Conditions**" page.

To create these pages, log into your WordPress dashboard and click the "Pages" tab. This will expand the list and you'll see the words "Add New."

After you click the "**Add New**" link, you'll be prompted to enter a title for your new page. There'll also be a section below the title where you can add your text.

Start by adding an "**About Us**" page. Enter the words *About Us* in the title section and just enter some sample text in the section below. You can add all your information in this section later after you finish this chapter.

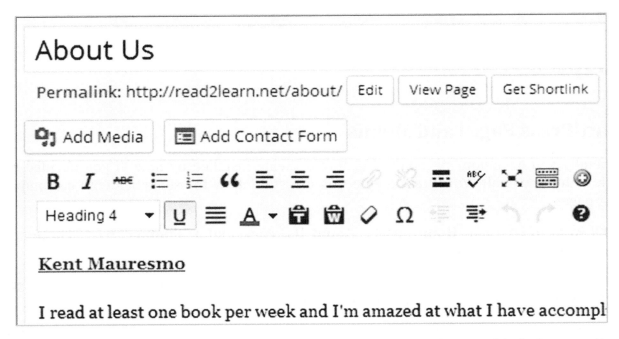

Now click the button on right side of the page that says "**Publish**" to publish the page live. Next click the "**View Page**" button and you'll see a sample of your "About Us" page.

You'll notice that the "About Us" page that you've created now appears in your navigation menu on your website. Repeat this step for the other pages that you want to create for your website. If the page that you created doesn't show up on your navigation menu, I'll show you how to fix this later.

TIP: If you purchased a theme that came with "*Demo*" content, then this process will be a lot easier for you. Just upload the demo content (per your themes instructions), and most the pages you need will already be created for you. You can just edit the pages and enter in your information.

Link to Homepage

Creating a link to your home page is a different depending on your website theme. Some themes come with a link to your home page, and some other themes don't.

If your theme doesn't come with a "Home" page link then you need to create one. To create a link that links back to your homepage, you need to click the "**Appearance**" tab on your dashboard to expand the menu. Next you'll need to click the link that says "**Menus**" and you'll be taken to a page where you can customize your navigation menus for your website.

Depending on your theme, you *might* have to create your first menu manually, but it's easy. At the top of the screen you'll see a link that says "create a new menu."

Click on that link, and give your menu a name. You can simply name it "main menu." After the menu is created, you can add your homepage link.

You should see a section that says "**Links.**" Click on that section to expand all the available options. Next, enter your homepage URL in the section that says "URL." Within the "Link Text" box write the words "Home" or "Homepage." (see the next image.)

Now click the button that says "**Add to Menu**" and this will add a homepage link to your navigation menu.

If the other pages you've created earlier aren't showing up on your navigation menu, then you can fix that within this section on your dashboard. You'll see a section on this page that says "**Pages**." This box contains all the pages that you've created for your website.

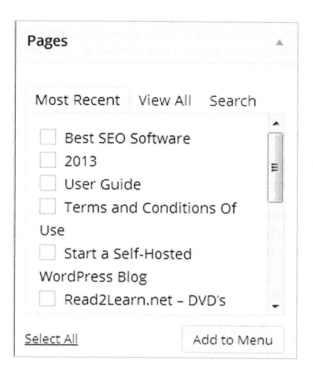

Check the box next to the pages that you'd like to add to your navigation menu. Next just click the "**Add to Menu**" button to add these pages to your navigation menu.

As you add the pages, you should see them appear in the box on the right. If there's a page in that box that you don't want to show on your websites menu bar (you want a hidden page), then click the drop-down arrow and click the link that says "**Remove**."

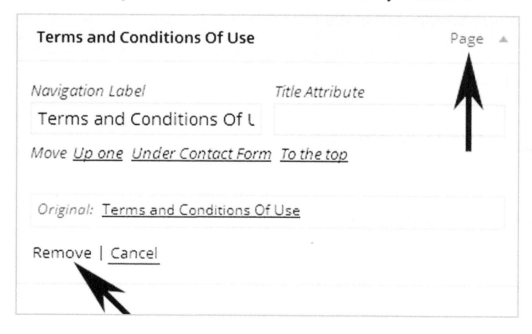

Clicking "remove" only removes the page from your websites menu and it doesn't delete the page. After you've added all the pages that you'd like to show on your menu, you can start to **arrange these pages**.

For example, you'll probably want your "Homepage" to be the first tab on your websites navigation menu. To accomplish this, just click on the "Homepage" tab that you created earlier (click and hold down on your mouse) and **drag** the homepage tab to the top spot.

If you want the "About Us" page to be the second tab on your websites menu, then click and drag that tab under the "Homepage."

If you have a lot of pages, then you can <u>create submenus</u> as well. If you need to create a submenu, drag the tab slightly to the *right* under the main menu it belongs to. Look at the image below to see what I'm talking about.

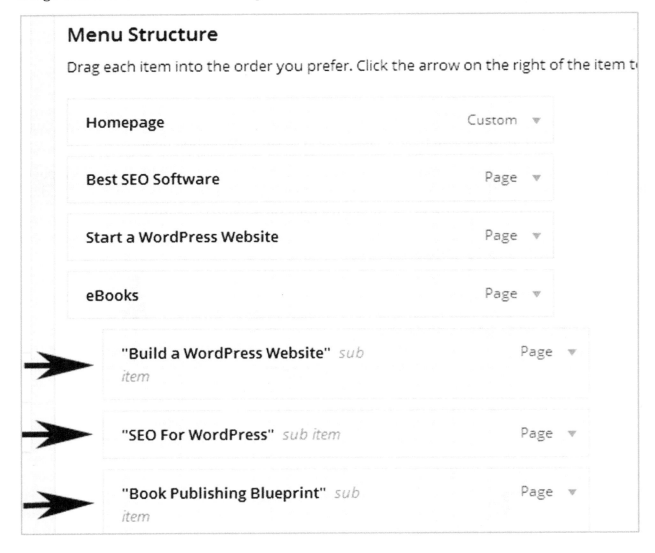

After you're satisfied with the order of your menu, click the button on the bottom right that says "**Save Menu.**" Now if you visit your homepage, you'll see your navigation menus in the appropriate order.

Theme Options

Go back into your Wordpress dashboard and click on "**Appearances**." When the list expands you should see a link that says, "**Theme Options.**" Click on that link to customize your theme.

If you're using the default Wordpress theme, then you might not see this option. If you have a premium theme, then you'll see this option for sure.

Since every premium theme is different, I'll just give you an idea of what some of your theme options _might_ be based on my theme.

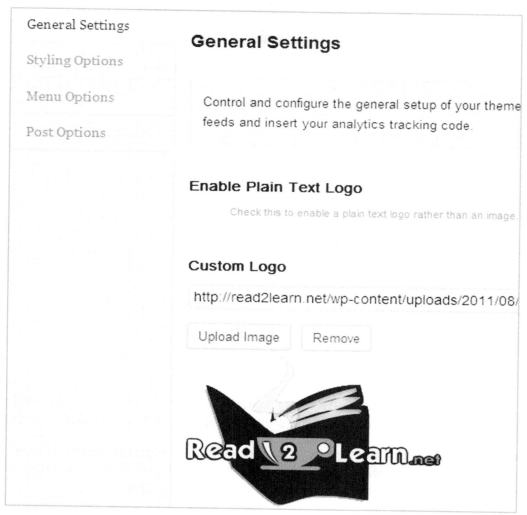

Some of my theme options allow me to upload a custom <u>logo</u>, custom <u>favicon</u>, and there's a section to paste some code for <u>Google Analytics</u> to track my website visitors.

I highly recommend that you purchase some type of logo software and make your own logo. It doesn't make sense to pay a graphic designer $100 to make *ONE* logo when you can buy software for $50 and make **unlimited** logos yourself.

You can Google *"Free Favicons"* to find a free favicon that matches your websites theme. You can also just upload your logo into the favicon section and it will shrink your logo to size. If you do not know what a favicon is, look at the next image.

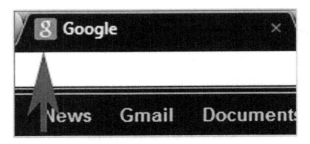

That tiny image in the address bar next to Google's URL is a favicon. Don't waste too much time trying to craft the perfect favicon because it's not that important. The logo on your website is more important because it symbolizes your brand.

Next, you'll also notice that I have an option to enter some Google analytics code on my theme.

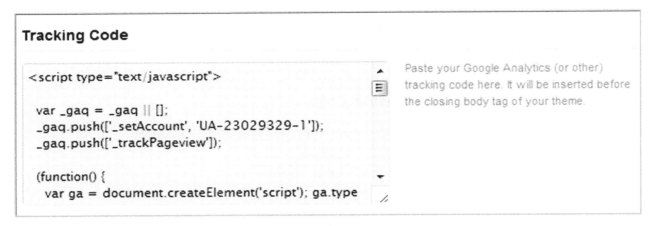

You can get your personalized Google Analytics code by creating an account at <u>www.google.com/analytics</u>. Just follow the step-by-step instructions on Google's website.

There are a lot of premium themes that'll allow you to change the color scheme of your website too. **Each theme is different**, so your theme options will be completely different from mine. Just play around with your theme to figure out how it works!

If you decide to purchase a really fancy and/or complicated theme, then I'm 90% sure that your theme will come with <u>instructions</u> and a <u>support forum</u>. I had to visit the support forum for my theme when I first got started too.

In the next chapter I'll show you how to use the "**widgets**" function of your website. Widgets allow you to customize the sidebar and footer areas on your website.

Chapter 5

Custom Sidebar

To customize your sidebar you need to log into your Dashboard and click the "Appearance" tab. This will expand that list and you'll see a link that says "**Widgets.**"

After you click "Widgets" you'll be taken to a page that's full of available widgets that you can add to your sidebar. You'll see the options to add categories, archives, latest tweets, flickr photos, banner ads, blogroll, RSS feeds, and anything else you can think of.

Widgets				
Available Widgets			**Main Sidebar**	**Footer Area 2**
Archives	Add	Blog Subscription... Add	Text Edit	
A monthly archive of your site's Posts.		Add an email signup form to allow people to subscribe to your blog.	Custom Tabbed Widget Edit	**Footer Area 3**
Calendar	Add	Categories Add	Text Edit	**Footer Area 4**
A calendar of your site's Posts.		A list or dropdown of categories.	Image (Jetpack) Edit	
Custom 125x125 ...	Add	Custom 250x250 Ad Add	Image (Jetpack) Edit	

You should keep your website as user friendly as possible, so try not to add too many widgets to your sidebar. For example, do you really need to add a calendar to your sidebar? Probably not!

My recommendation is to use the "**Recent Posts**" widget and the "**Recent Comments**" widget. Your sidebar is also a good place to add links to your Facebook and Twitter accounts if you have one.

If you're building an email list then it's a good idea to add an email subscriber box to your sidebar too. Just make sure that your sidebar isn't overwhelming because it'll distract people away from your website content.

To add a widget that you want, just click the words "**Add**" on the top right corner of the widget. That'll take you to a page that'll give you several placement options for your widget. If you don't have the words "Add" on your widgets, then that means that you can **drag the widgets** wherever you want them to go. (Main sidebar, page sidebar, footer area.)

The **main sidebar** and the **page sidebar** are completely different. The main sidebar will only display widgets on your homepage. The page sidebar will only show your widgets on other pages you've created like your "About Us" page. When you're done adding your widgets, you can check to see how they look by viewing your homepage.

Edit Your Widgets the Easy Way

I'll give you a tip to make the editing process easier so you don't have to keep navigating back to the widgets section in your dashboard to make changes.

On the widgets page, you'll notice the name of your website at the top-left of the page. That's actually a clickable link that will take you to your homepage.

Right Click on that link and you'll have the option to open the link in a new tab. After you open this link in a new tab, you'll be able to view your homepage in a separate tab within your web browser.

You should have **two tabs open** now. One tab should display your widgets, and the other tab should display your homepage. If you want to see how your new changes look, just click on your homepage tab and click the *refresh* button on your web browser. If you don't like the way your widgets look, then just click back over to the widgets tab and make the adjustments.

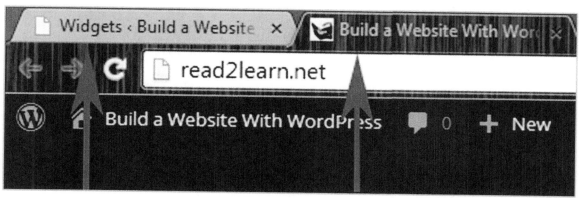

This will save you a lot of time compared to manually clicking back in forth from your homepage to your widgets dashboard. I hope that makes sense and I didn't confuse you.

Footers & HTML Code

You can also add widgets to your footer area which is at the bottom of your website. I used to have some widgets in my footer, but I deleted them. I personally didn't like the way it looked on my website.

TIP: If you're not sure which widgets you want to add, just check out some other websites that you admire and copy their layout. Just remember to keep your sidebar simple and you'll be fine.

A lot of 3rd party websites will give you **HTML code** to display image links on your site. If you want to add HTML code to your sidebar, then use the widget that says "**Text**."

If you want to use custom *Twitter* and *Facebook* icons on your website, then go to www.sixrevisions.com/category/freebies. That's a very popular design blog, and they have a lot of custom "social icons" that you can download for free.

Look at the image below to see an example of one of the free icon sets available at **Sixrevisions**! Make sure to check out their website if you have time.

Social Sketches: Exclusive Free Hand-Sketched Icon Set

Jan 9 2010 by **An Phan Van** | 🗨 59 Comments

continue reading »

I have a video on my website showing you how to upload these icon sets. It's really easy and you have to use the "**Text**" widget to paste some simple HTML code. You can find the video here: http://read2learn.net/upload-six-revisions-free-icon-sets.

Your new website should be coming along nicely if you've been following everything I've showed you. Even though your blog now looks better than 90% of the websites online, we still have a few more things to cover.

In the next chapter, I'll show you how to optimize the "User" and "Settings" tab within your dashboard. You're almost ready to create your first blog post!

Chapter 6.

User Settings

Log into your Wordpress dashboard, and you'll see the word "**Users**" on the left column. Click on "Users" to expand the menu.

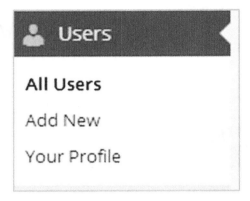

The "Users" settings will allow you to give other users access to your website. If you have more than one author for your website, then you can set them up with a username and password by clicking "**Add New**."

Add New User

IMPORTANT: You need to select the correct "Role" of each user account that you add. The new user account can be an <u>Administrator</u>, <u>Editor</u>, <u>Author</u>, etc.

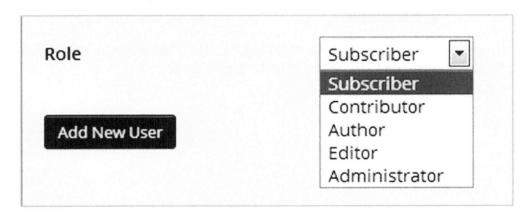

Keep in mind that the "Administrator" role can make can make major changes to your website. So if you decide to add a new user, you might want to set their role as an "**Author**" so they'll have limited access to your website.

Since you're just starting out, don't worry about adding new users. This feature might come in handy later if you decide to have "guest bloggers" write content on your website.

Personal Options

Click the link that says "**Your Profile**" under the "User" settings. The first section on this page will show your "Personal Options." You have the ability to change your Visual Editor, Color Scheme, Keyboard Shortcuts, Proofreading options, and English options.

You can play with these options if you want, but I highly recommend that you leave the default settings the way they are.

The next section below says "**Name**." You need to make some changes to this section.

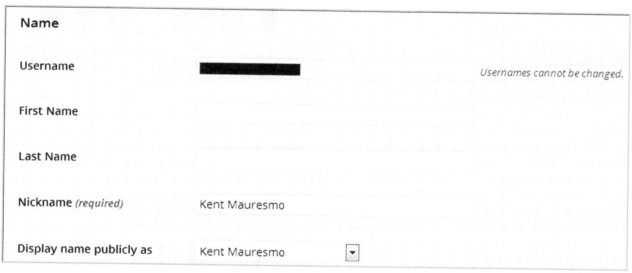

The "Username" cannot be changed. This is the same username you picked when you set up your hosting account with Bluehost. It's also the same username you use to sign into your WordPress administration area.

Below your username, you'll have the option to add your first name, last name, and a nickname. The "**nickname**" you choose will show up as the author of your blog posts and articles, so pick an appropriate nickname.

For example, my nickname is "*Kent Mauresmo*", so you'll notice that all my blog posts show the author as "Kent Mauresmo." You can see this in the image below which shows that I'm the author of the article.

IMPORTANT: Your "nickname" should be different from your "username." I'm telling you this for a good reason. Notice that under the nickname section, it says "Display name publicly as" and you'll see a drop down menu.

Display name publicly as	Kent Mauresmo ▾

The drop down menu will give you the option to display your "username" or your "nickname." Make sure that you select the "nickname" that you just created.

You don't want to publicly display your "username." Hackers try to break into websites all the time. If you display your username publicly, then hackers only have to guess your password.

Your username is the same name that you use to log into your WordPress dashboard. So it's very important that you keep your **username** *and* **password** as secure as possible.

Contact Info

The next section is for your contact info. The only information *required* is your email address. Bluehost will give you a free email address when you purchase a hosting package with them.

Contact Info

E-mail *(required)*	contact@read2learn.net
Website	http://read2learn.net
AIM	

If you want to be **100% professional**, then you should use an email address that's attached to your domain. That's why my email address is contact@read2learn.net . You can create a professional email address by clicking the "webmail" icon within your hosting account. If you need help, then contact your web host.

About Yourself

The next section is "About Yourself." You can enter a short bio about yourself in this section.

About Yourself

| Biographical Info | Thank you for taking the time to read this article! We appreciate you and we want to thank you for your support. Please link back to us. and lets connect on Twitter! I'll see you there. -<a href="https://plus.google.com/109483891577856451449? rel=author">Kent Mauresmo+</a>. |

Share a little biographical information to fill out your profile. This may be shown publicly.

Depending on your theme, you'll have the option to show this Bio under your blog posts. For example, if I click "Appearances" on my dashboard and click "Theme Options", I have the option to show "Author Bios" for each blog post.

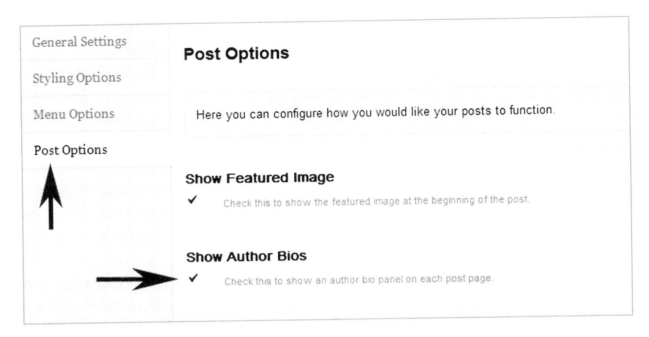

Depending on your theme, you may or may not have this option. If you look at the image below, you'll see an example of what the "Author Bio" looks like under my blog posts.

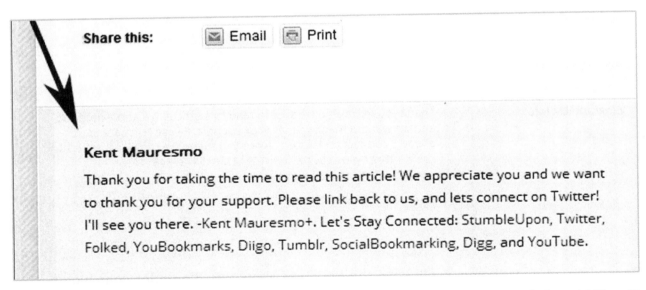

After you finish with your bio, you have the option to change your password if you'd like. If you change or reset your password, the information will be sent to the email address in the "Contact Info" section. If you don't want to change your password, then leave this section blank.

New Password

If you would like to change the password type a new one. Otherwise leave this blank.

Repeat New Password

Type your new password again.

Strength indicator

Hint: The password should be at least seven c
letters, numbers and symbols like ! " ? $ % ^ &

Update Profile

Check to make sure that your profile is filled out correctly. If everything looks good, then click the blue button that says "**Update Profile**" and you're done! Now you know everything about the "User" section of Wordpress.

In the next chapter, I'll show you how to customize your "General Settings." After we complete the general settings, you'll be ready to create your first blog post or article.

Chapter 7.

Settings

Changing your general settings in Wordpress is very easy. Log into your WordPress Dashboard and click the "Settings" tab on the left column.

After you click the settings tab, it'll expand a list of settings that you can change within Wordpress. The first setting you can change are the "**General**" settings.

General Settings

The general settings will give you the option to add a Site Title, Tagline, Wordpress Address, Site Address, and Email address.

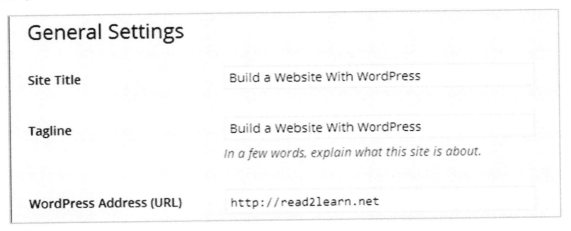

For your Site Title, you should enter your main keyword phrase. If your website is about training poodles, then you should enter "*How To Train Poodles*" in the site title area. You can enter the same keyword into the "Tagline" section if you'd like.

Enter your domain name in the "Wordpress Address" & "Site Address" section. For the email section, enter your primary email address that you'll use for this website.

You can skip the "membership" and "new user default role" section. The default settings for this section are fine. Next just set your time zone, date format, and time format; and click "**Save Changes**" on the bottom left.

Now go back to the settings tab and click the "**Writing**" link.

Writing Settings

The writing settings will give you the option to change the size of the post box, formatting, default post category, and default link category.

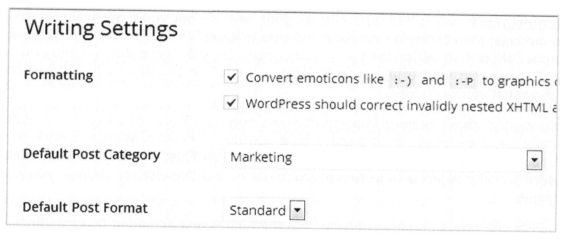

Next to the "formatting" section, click the two check boxes. One box is to convert emoticons into graphics like this → ☺, and the next box helps correct errors on your website.

Since you're just starting out, I would leave everything else in the "writing" settings as is! Most of these setting can be adjusted when you write your articles.

Click "**Save Changes**" and go back to the settings tab and click the "Reading" link.

Reading Settings

The reading settings are very important because this is where you set your homepage. If you're website is mainly a blog, then check the box that says "Your latest posts." This will place your blog as your homepage.

Reading Settings

Front page displays ⟶ ● Your latest posts

○ A <u>static page</u> (select below)

Front page: — Select — ▾

Posts page: — Select — ▾

<u>What If You Don't Want a Blog For Your Homepage?</u>

If you want to set a specific page as your homepage, then click the option that says "static page." Click the drop down arrow and select a page from the list to set as your homepage. You'll have to create the page first in order to see it within the drop down list.

<u>Very Important</u>: If you still want a blog on your website but you don't want the blog on your homepage; then create a new page and title it "Blog." If you look at the image above, you'll notice there's an option for your "posts page." Click the drop down menu and select the "Blog" page that you've just created. This will run the WordPress *blog script* on the "Blog" page that you've created.

The information above is very important! Some newbie's have raised concerns that our books only show people how to build a blog and not a website. With one click of your mouse, you can **remove the blog** from your homepage and just create static pages instead. A standard website is just a collection of static pages, and I've already showed you how to create pages.

I'm showing you how to build a website, and the blog is just an added feature. Blogs <u>rank higher</u> within Google because Google knows that blogs are consistently updated. Search engines strive to provide users with the most current up to date information.

Later in this book I'm going to show you how to create blog posts, but you can use the same information to create static pages. The dashboard used to create blog posts and static pages is <u>exactly the same</u>.

Okay, now the next option within the "reading settings" is to select how many blog posts to show on your homepage. I have mine set to 5 blog posts so my website loads faster.

That's all you need to change for now. You can leave everything else the way it is. Click **"Saving Changes"** and move on to the next settings which will be the "Discussion" settings.

Discussion Settings

You can customize your default article settings, and comment settings. All these settings are self-explanatory, so you can change this however you'd like. The default settings are pretty good, so you can just leave everything the way it is.

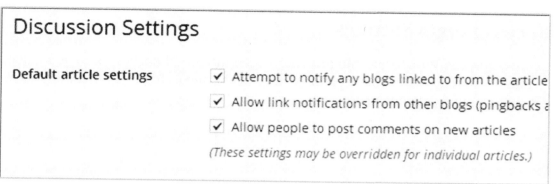

There is one section that says, "**Before a comment appears**." It's a good idea to check the box that says *"Comment author must have a previously approved comment."* This will automatically approve comments from someone that you've approved in the past.

All new comments will have to be approved by you before they're displayed on your website. This will prevent spam comments from being displayed on your blog.

Next, scroll down and you'll see a section for "Avatars." I spoke about this earlier, but as a recap, you can choose to show or not show avatars (Gravatars) on your blog.

If you decide to show avatars, make sure you set up the "default avatar" settings too. Here you can set a default avatar for people that don't have a registered Gravatar. The best option is to check the box that says "Gravatar Logo."

I personally don't show avatars on my site. I want people to focus on my websites content, and not all those little Gravatar pictures. Plus too many images can slow your website down, and I already have a lot of images on my page.

Click "**Save Changes**" on the bottom left hand corner. Next click "Media" under the settings tab.

Media Settings

Leave these settings exactly the way they are. I have never changed these settings and my website is fine. I don't know anyone that has changed the settings on this page. It's easier to change these dimensions within your blog posts as needed.

Click "**Save Changes**" and click *Permalinks* under the settings tab.

Permalink Settings

Under the permalink settings, you will have "common settings" and "optional settings." You only want to make changes to the common settings area. Choose the "**Post name**" option and you're done. Click the "**Save Changes**" button.

Wordpress Plugin Settings

If you've installed the Wordpress plugins that I recommended earlier, then you'll see *some* of these plugins listed within the "**Settings**" tab. In the next chapter, I'll show you how to customize your plugin settings properly.

Chapter 8

Plugin Settings

In Chapter 2, I recommended several plugins to use for Wordpress. You'll have to configure some of these plugins or they won't work properly.

I'll show you step-by-step how to configure these plugins. Log into your Wordpress Dashboard and click the "**Settings**" tab. When you expand the list, you'll see general WordPress settings (general, writing, discussion, media, etc) and you'll see the plugins that you've installed earlier.

Find "**Metadata**" and click the link. This will take you to a page to customize your meta tags.

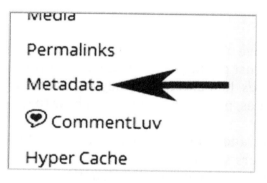

Meta Tags

"Front Page Descriptions" will allow you to influence how your homepage is described and displayed on search engines like Google. Whatever you enter into the *Front Page Description* section will be displayed on search engines describing your <u>homepage only</u>.

Ensure that your description is explicit and contains your most important keywords. So if your website is about "How to train your poodle", then make sure to use that phrase once or twice in your description. For example:

"Want to learn <u>how to train your poodle</u>? Learn <u>how to train your poodle</u> in 30 days or less with our video training course and eBook."

This will help trigger your website if someone types into Google, "how to train your poodle." Your site description should be between 150 and 250 characters.

Below the site description is a section for your "Front Page Keywords." Enter your most important keywords that are relevant to your website.

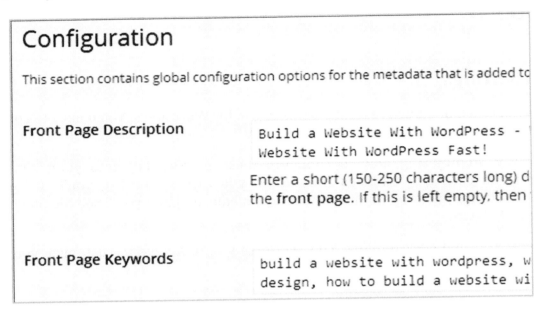

Search engine **spammers** have abused this meta keyword tag, so it has little benefit to your search engine rankings. I'm just giving you a "heads up" so you do not waste too much time with your *front page keywords*. Just enter a few keywords and separate them with commas. For example, "training poodles, poodle training, learn how to train my poodle, etc."

Next, scroll down the page and you'll see a few more options available to you. These options are for advanced users so don't worry about it. Leave everything else the way it is and click the "**Save Changes**" button at the bottom of the page.

On the top left of your dashboard, you'll see a link that says, "**All in One SEO**." Click that link so we can customize your SEO settings.

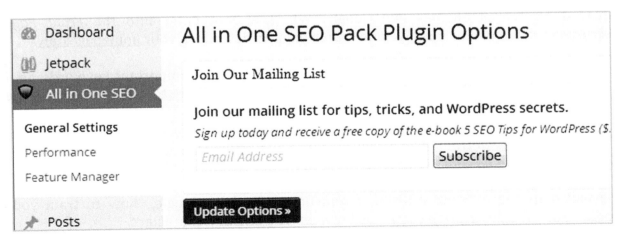

All in One SEO

SEO stands for *Search Engine Optimization*. In plain English, SEO means: "I want my website to appear on the first page of Google when people search for my keywords."

The first thing you'll notice about the *All in One SEO* plugin is that it looks very similar to the Meta Tags plugin. You can set up this plugin almost the same way. The only information you need to input into this plugin is your *Home Title, Home Description,* and *Home Keywords.*

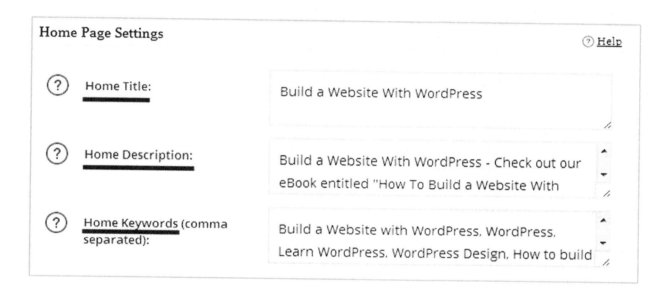

For your "**Home Title**", enter you most important keyword phrase in that section. You should enter your keyword phrase the same way people would enter it into search engines. If your website is about "Training Poodles", then your home title should be "How to Train Poodles" or something close to that.

For your "Home Description" and "Home Keywords", just **copy and paste** the same information that you entered into the "Meta Tags" plugin. You don't have to leave the "All in One SEO" page to do this. Navigate over to the settings tab and find the "Metadata" link. Now "right click" and open the Metadata page in a new tab.

You should now have 2 tabs open on your web browser. On the *Meta Tags* page, copy the "Site Description" text. (Right click in the description box and click the "Select All" option, then right click again and select "Copy.")

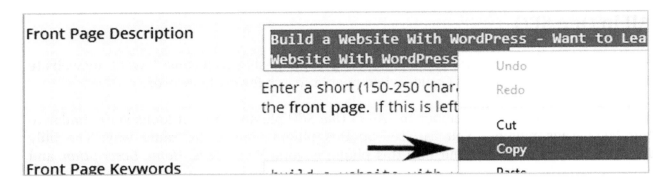

Navigate back to the *All in One SEO* tab. Place your mouse in the "Home Description" box and "Right Click" on your mouse. You'll see the option that says "Paste." Click on the "Paste" option to paste the copied text in this box.

Repeat this same step for the keywords. Copy the "Site Keywords" from the Meta Tags page, and paste them in the "Home Keywords" section on the *All in One SEO* page.

That's it! You're done with this plugin. If you have a *Google Plus* profile account and/or a *Google Webmasters* account; you'll have the option to link those accounts with the *All in One SEO* plugin too. You can customize the *All in One SEO* plugin further when you write your first blog post. I'll show you how to do that later.

Google XML Sitemaps

Under the settings tab, click the link that says "**XML-Sitemap**." On the plugin page, there should be a link that says "**build sitemap**." Just click that link and the plugin will build a sitemap for you.

You can scroll down the page to review the other options, but if you're not familiar with sitemaps then leave the settings the way they are. All the default options for this plugin are perfect.

Scroll down to the bottom of the page and click the "Update Options" button. Next, navigate back to the settings tab and click the "**Related Posts Thumbs**" link.

Related Posts Thumbnails

The default settings for this plugin are fine. You won't see this plugin in action until you get a few blog posts up. Once you have a few blog posts written on your website, you can come back and change the settings if you'd like.

The only changes I made were to the "Top text" section, and to the "Relation based on" section. I changed the top text settings to say "**Related Posts You'll Like**" and I changed the relation based settings to "**Random.**"

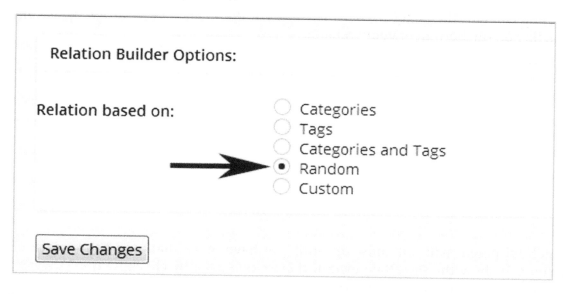

Click "Save" Changes" when you're done with this plugin. Take a look at the image below to see how this plugin will look on your website **after** you have a few blog posts up!

Now navigate back over to the settings tab. Find that link that says "**PageNavi**" and click it. We're going to take a look at some of the settings for this cool plugin.

PageNavi Settings

The default settings to PageNavi are fine. As your website grows and you publish more articles, you can edit the PageNavi settings. Look at the image below to see what PageNavi will look like on the bottom of your website.

The PageNavi plugin will not show up until you have more than one *page* worth of blog posts. You can show the PageNavi even if there's one page by checking the "Always Show Page Navigation" within the setting area for this plugin.

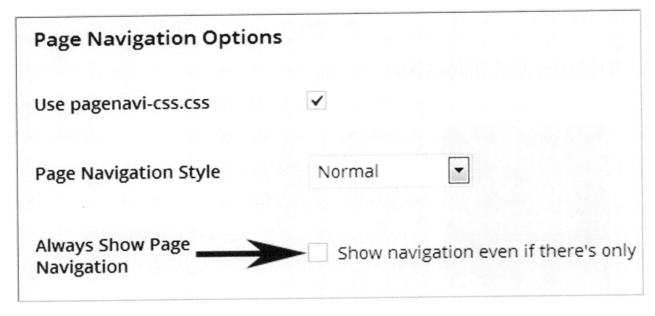

Review all the options so you're familiar with the plugin, and click "**Save Changes**" on the bottom left. Navigate back over to the settings tab area. Under the settings tab, you'll see a tab that says "**WPB2D.**" That's your "WordPress Backup to Dropbox" plugin! Click that link to get started with the plugin.

WordPress Backup to Dropbox Plugin

For this plugin to work, you'll need to create a free dropbox account. The website is www.dropbox.com. You can create a dropbox account by clicking the "sign in" link on the top right corner of their website.

There's also a video on their homepage that you can watch. The video will explain how dropbox works if you need more information. After you create your account, log into WordPress and click the tab that says "**WPB2D**" under the settings tab.

After you click the tab, you'll be taken to a page that'll ask you to authorize your dropbox account with your website. Click the authorize button to sync your dropbox account with your website.

The settings for this plugin are very simple. The only important setting you might want to change is the frequency settings. This setting will allow you to set how often your website is backed up into Dropbox. By default, I believe it's set to "weekly" but you can change it to daily if you'd like.

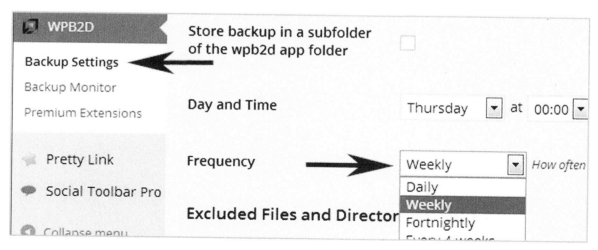

The final step is to click the "**Backup Now**" link. This will prompt you to backup all the files on your website into a secure folder on your desktop. Your backup files will also be made available at Dropbox.com! So if your website crashes and then your computer explodes, all your files will remain safe and secure on Dropbox's server.

The next plugin you need to set up is "Shareaholic." This is a social sharing plugin that'll allow people to share your articles on Facebook, Twitter, Pinterest, and a lot more. Click the "Shareaholic" tab to customize this plugin.

Shareaholic Plugin (Sexy Bookmarks)

This plugin is fun and easy to set up! After you click the Shareaholic tab, you'll see a link under it that says *Available Apps.* Click that link and you'll have the option to choose where you want your "Share Buttons" to be displayed.

You can display your "Share Buttons" on each individual post, your pages, index, and categories. The best place to display your share buttons are on your posts and pages. You can choose where to display your share buttons by checking or un-checking the box next to the Post, Page, Index, and Category options.

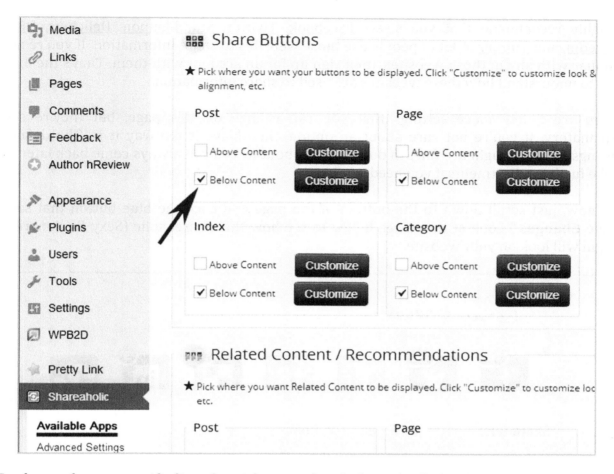

To choose from a specific list of social networks, click on the "Edit" button. By default, the most popular social networks are already chosen for you. You can remove the networks you don't want by clicking the "x" on the top left of the icon. You can add networks by clicking on the icons from the available list.

I highly recommend that you select <u>Facebook</u>, <u>Twitter</u>, <u>Stumbleupon</u>, <u>Delicious</u>, <u>Digg</u>, <u>Linkedin</u>, and <u>Tumblr</u>. A lot of people use those websites to share information. If you're not familiar with any of those websites, then sign up for an account with them. That's the only way to understand how these websites are used to share information.

There are a few more settings that you can change on this page, but they're self explanatory. If you're not sure about an option, then leave it the way it is. The default settings for this plugin are fine, so don't worry about it. You can always come back later to make further adjustments if you need too.

For now, just scroll down to the bottom of the page and click the blue button that says "**Save Changes**." Look at the image below to see how this Shareaholic (Sexy Bookmarks) plugin will look on your website.

You don't have to use this particular plugin if you don't like it. There are a lot of plugins that you can use that'll allow you to share your website via social networks. If you'd like to explore more options, then search for "social sharing" when you're looking for WordPress plugins.

It's also important to note that some professional WordPress themes will already have social sharing buttons. So depending on your theme, you may not need to install "share" buttons.

WP Maintenance Plugin

You only need to activate this plugin if you're going to use it. To activate this plugin and/or adjust the settings, you need to click your "**Plugins**" tab and find it in your list of plugins. If the plugin is already activated, then just click the "<u>Settings</u>" option under the plugin.

In the drop down menu, you'll see the options *True* and *False*. If you set this to *True*, then you'll activate your maintenance mode page. If you leave this set to *False*, then your maintenance mode page won't show.

Most of the other settings for this plugin are fine. One notable feature is that you can **change the theme** of your maintenance splash page. Keep in mind that you'll only see the maintenance page if you're logged out of your dashboard! So instead of logging in and out 10 times to see which page looks the best, just pick the "**Chemistry**" theme. It looks really professional and it gets the job done!

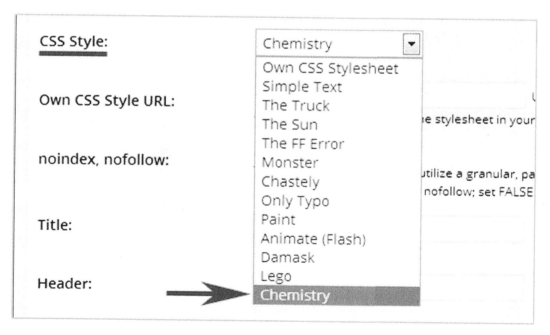

Click the "**Save**" button at the bottom of the plugin settings to save your changes. Now everybody that visits your website will see your *Maintenance Mode* splash page. Since you're the administrator, you'll still be able to see your entire website unless you log out of your dashboard.

This plugin is really useful if you purchase a new theme and you need time to reorganize your website. When your website is ready to go live, the easiest way to turn off the maintenance splash page is to click the "**deactivate**" link under the plugin. If you need to use the plugin again in the future, then just click the "activate" link to activate the Maintenance page again.

Hyper Cache

This is a very simple cache plugin that anybody can use. There are other cache plugins, but they have a lot of bugs, or they're too complicated to set up. I tried almost all of them, so trust me when I say this cache plugin is the most user-friendly. Cache plugins will help your **website load faster**.

For this plugin to work, you'll have to log into your hosting account and add a line of code to your WordPress file. I have a video on my website showing you how to do it. Here's the link to the video: http://read2learn.net/hyper-cache. If you still have questions about setting up this plugin, then send me an email and I'll help you out.

Next, I'll review the "Jetpack" plugin. The Jetpack plugin is located near the top of the page below the *Dashboard* tab. Click it.

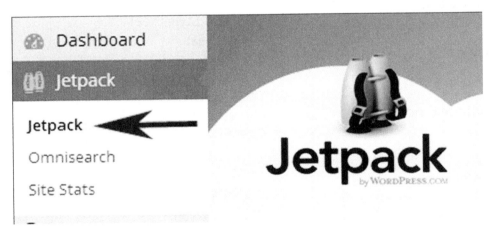

Jetpack Plugin

The jetpack plugin is exactly as the name implies; it's a pack! It's currently a pack of 28 plugins as I write this book. Each plugin will have a button under it that'll say **Activate**, **Learn More** or **Configure**. If you're not sure what a plugin does, just click the "Learn More" button.

There are two plugins that I want to go over with you within Jetpack. The first plugin is titled "Sharing." This plugin will allow you to share your blog post the same way as the Shareaholic plugin.

Since you're already using "Shareaholic", it's not necessary to add more Twitter and Facebook buttons on your blog. What this plugin is excellent for is adding an "Email" and "Print" button at the bottom of your blog post.

Some people like to print articles or email them to their friends. So click the configure button under the "Sharing" plugin.

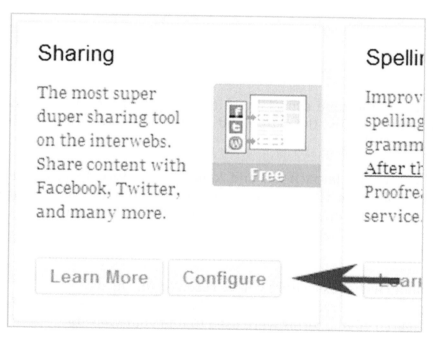

Next you'll see a box with a list of available services. Below that you'll see another box that says "Enabled Services." Click and drag the **Email** icon, and **Print** icon down to "Enabled Services." Click "Saved Changes" at the bottom of this page. Now your website visitors will have the option to print or email your blog posts.

I print out articles all the time especially if it's a *"How To"* article. I always look for the **"Print"** icon so I can print just the *article* and not the entire website. This is a very useful feature, so don't overlook it.

Next, navigate back to the Jetpack tab and look for the **"Wordpress.com Stats"** plugin. Make sure that this plugin is activated! You can also click the "configure" button under this plugin to see what your options are, but the default settings are good.

This plugin will tell you:

- How many websites visitors you've received for the day
- How people were referred to your website (Google, Bing, Yahoo, Forums, etc.)
- What search engine terms were used to find your website
- Which blog post or page did people view the most
- Which links were clicked on your website, and how many times

To view your site stats, just click the link under the JetPack tab that says **"Site Stats."**

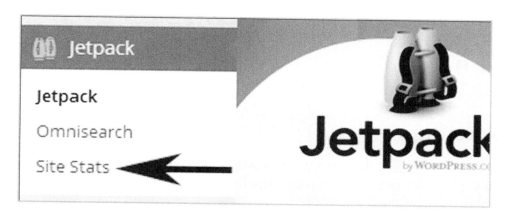

Most of the other Jetpack plugins should already be activated. The only thing you need to do is configure the plugins based on your needs. If a Jetpack plugin needs to be activated, then you'll see a button that says "**Activate**" under the plugin.

If you're not sure what a plugin does, just click the "**Learn More**" button under the plugin for a detailed explanation. Sometimes they'll even show you a video within the "learn more" section. You'll have a better understanding of how these plugins work as you start to create articles for your website.

We're all done with these plugins, so let's create your first blog post! In the next chapter, I'll show you how to use WordPress to create articles that your readers and search engines will love.

Chapter 9.

Blog Post Settings

To write your first blog post, log into your Wordpress dashboard. On the dashboard, you'll see the "**Posts**" tab. Click that tab to expand the list, and you'll see several options.

Click the option that says "**Add New**" and you'll be taken to a page where you can enter a "Title" and content for your blog.

This is the most important part of the book so pay close attention. If you follow my advice, you'll make your readers happy, and your website will rank higher with Google.

Blog Post Title

Some bloggers recommend that you use a "Surefire Blog Post Title That Will Suck Your Readers in like a Black-hole from Star Wars!" If you write *"over the top"* titles like that just to attract attention, then you better deliver above average content.

People search the internet looking for **specific information** or products, not hype. Writing extravagant blog post titles might attract website visitors, but if your content is poor then you'll just end up with frustrated users.

So what's my suggestion? Title your blog post articles the **same way** people search for information using Google. No one will type into Google, "Surefire Blog Post Titles That Will Suck Your Readers in like a Black-hole from Star Wars!" But they might type, *"Good Blog Post Titles"* or *"How to Write Good Blog Posts."*

The closer your blog title matches a search query, the better chance you'll have of showing up on the first page of Google.

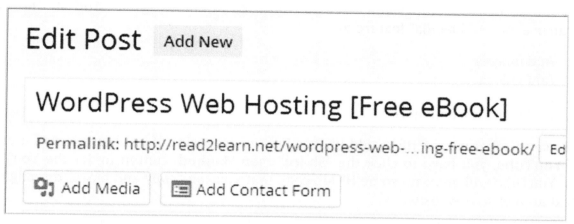

Also your blog title is your **H1 tag** for your article. If you don't know what an H1 tag is, don't panic. All you need to know is that search engines look at the H1 tag (your title) to decide if your article is relevant to search results.

So use clear keyword phrases in your title! Leave out the "Star Wars Black-hole" nonsense unless your blog post is about Star Wars and Black-holes.

Permalink

Directly below the "Title" you'll see the words "**Permalink**." After you enter your title, WordPress will add a default permalink for you. You can edit your permalink by clicking the edit button.

I always edit my permalinks! I recommend that you edit your permalinks too to match your title exactly. So if the title of your blog post is, "*How To Write Good Blog Posts*", then you should edit your permalink and enter the text: **how-to-write-good-blog-posts**

Your permalinks show up in the Google search results. If your permalink and title match exactly, then you'll increase the chance of your article showing up on page #1 of Google for that specific search term.

Add Media Files

Below the permalink settings you'll see an icon used to manage your "**Add Media**" files. You can use the "Add Media" feature to:

1. Add images.
2. Add videos.
3. Add audio.
4. Add PDF files, and more.

You'll use this feature <u>mostly to add images</u> into your articles. If you want to add a video from **YouTube**, you have to click the **"Share"** then **"Embed"** button under the YouTube video. YouTube will give you some HTML code that you can "copy and paste" directly into the text area of your website.

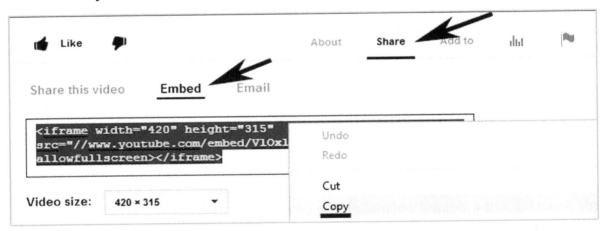

For the video to work on your website, you'll need to click over to the "**TEXT**" tab while creating your article. If you paste the HTML code into the "Visual" tab, then the video won't show up on your website.

Toolbar

Below the "Add Media" icon, you'll see a toolbar. This toolbar looks similar to *Microsoft Word*, and you can use this toolbar to bold text, use italics, bullet points, etc. If you're not sure what a toolbar option does, then just hover your mouse over it.

You've probably noticed that most websites only show a snippet of a blog post. To continue reading the post, you usually have to click a link that says "*Continue Reading*" or "*Read Full Article.*"

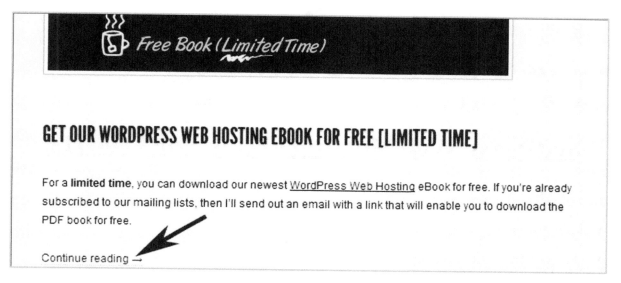

If you'd like to only show a sample of your blog post this way, then use the "**Insert More Tag**" on the toolbar.

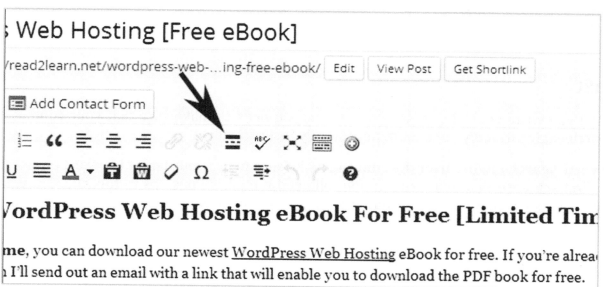

The second to last button on the toolbar is called *"Show/Hide Kitchen Sink."* I have no idea why it's called that, but click that button to **expand your toolbar options**.

Now you'll notice <u>additional options</u> on your toolbar like:

- Format (default is paragraph.)
- Underline
- Text color
- Paste from WORD (Microsoft Word.)
- Custom Characters
- Undo
- Help, etc.

Text

When you write your blog posts and articles, you need to make sure that your content is "search engine friendly", and more importantly "user friendly."

To write **search engine friendly content**, make sure to use your target keyword phrase in the first sentence that you write. If you followed the previous steps in this chapter, your blog <u>title</u>, <u>permalink</u>, and now your <u>first sentence</u> should have the same exact keyword phrase.

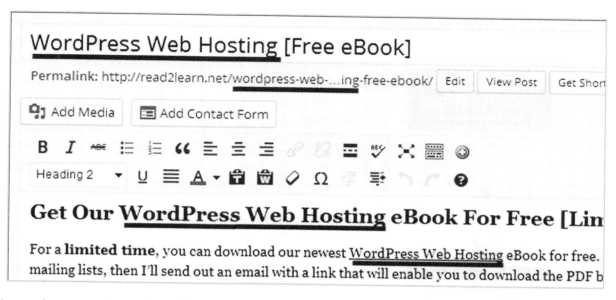

Now when search engines like Google come to scan your article, your article will rank a lot higher than most of your competition. Google looks at the **Title** of your article, the **first few sentences** of your article, and the **permalink** of the article. That's why you want to make sure your keyword phrase matches exactly in those 3 areas of your article.

Depending on the length of your article, you should add your exact keyword phrase a few more times throughout your article.

WARNING: Do not stuff your blog articles with keywords in every other sentence! That's what's known as a splog (Spam Blog.) Keep in mind that your readers are more important than the search engines.

To write **user friendly** content for your readers you need to:

1. Write small paragraphs (2 – 4 sentences max.)
2. Insert pictures throughout your articles.
3. Use bullet points, bold type, italics, and underlined text.

Look at image below for an example:

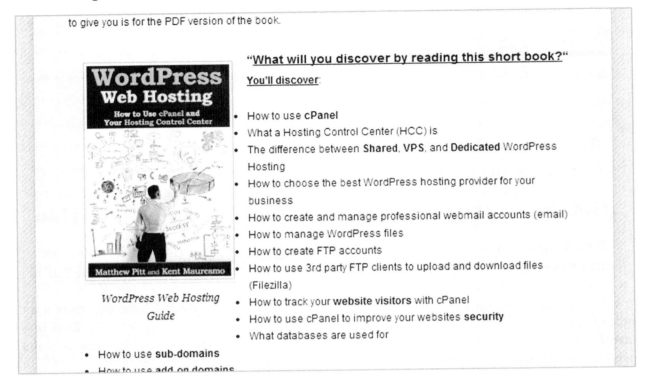

Metadata

After you're finished writing your article, scroll down until you see the Metadata section. Within the Metadata section, you'll see different areas where you can enter the following information:

- Description
- Keywords
- Title
- News Keywords
- Full Meta Tags (leave this section blank)

Metadata

Description:

WordPress Web Hosting [Free Book] - Get a copy of our WordPres:
Time Offer...

Enter a custom description of 30-50 words (based on an average word length of 5 char

If the *description* field is left blank, a *description* meta tag will be **automatically** genera
set, directly from the first paragraph of the content.

Keywords:

wordpress web hosting free book, wordpress ebook, best wordpres:

If you're constructing your articles the way I've recommended; then the title and first paragraph of your articles are already optimized for search engines. Just copy your title and paste it into the "title" field; and copy the first two sentences of your article and paste it into the "description field."

When you're entering your *Keywords* and *News Keywords*, don't forget to enter your most important keyword **first**. Leave the "Full Meta Tag" section blank. If you enter keywords into this section, I've noticed that your keywords will show up on the top left corner of your website and it looks weird.

All in One SEO Pack

Scroll down past the Metadata section and you'll see your "**All in One Seo Pack**" setting for your article. You have the option to customize your SEO settings for each page/blog post that you write. You'll notice that the *All in One SEO* settings look very similar to the Metadata settings.

You have the option to enter a **Title**, **Description**, and **Keywords**. Whatever information you enter into this section is exactly how it'll be displayed in the search engines. These settings will override your actual blog title within the search engines.

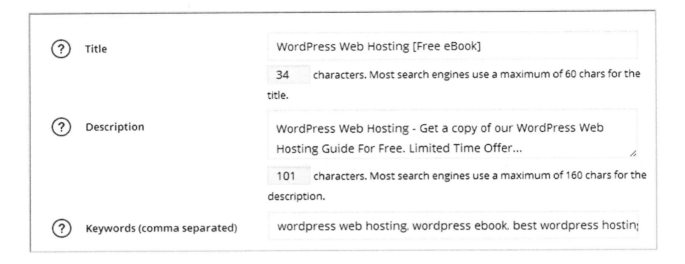

Let's say that your actual blog title is, *"**Learn How to Blog**."* If you decide to enter "***Win a Million Dollars***" in the title settings for *All in One SEO*, then Google will display "***Win a Million Dollars***" for the title of your article. I know people that enter misleading stuff like this just for extra website visitors, but don't do that.

To use this plugin correctly:

1. Enter the **same title** as your blog article.
2. Copy and paste the first few sentences of your blog post into the description section.
3. Enter your main keyword phrase into the keyword section. You don't need to add a huge list of keywords there. Just add your main keyword phrase once in the singular form, and once in the plural.

Categories, Tags, Featured Image

On the right side of the text box, you'll see a box that says *"Categories."* I suggest that you add a new category for each article/blog post. You can add a new category by clicking the *"Add New Category"* link below the categories box.

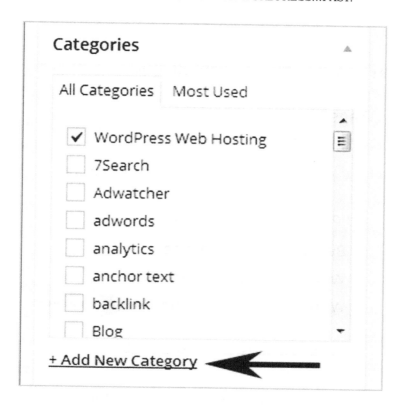

I like to add new categories that are an **exact match** to the title of my article. Now the article title, permalink, first paragraph, meta-tag plugin, All in One SEO plugin, and the categories section will all have the same exact keyword phrase.

The categories section might not seem important to most people, but take a look at the image below to see where the category information shows up on your blog. The categories are really important when it comes to Search Engine Optimization.

Tags

Below the categories section, you should see a section that says "Tags."

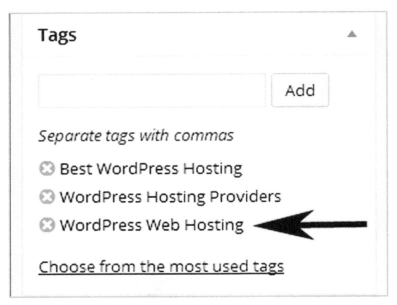

What I usually do here is copy the keyword phrases I used for the All in One SEO plugin, and paste those keywords into the "Tags" section. Click the "**Add**" button to add your tags.

Once again, do not stuff a lot of keywords into this section. The more keywords you add, the less weight each keyword will have. Just add a few keyword phrases to keep your article laser targeted.

Featured Image

My "Featured Image" option is below the tags section.

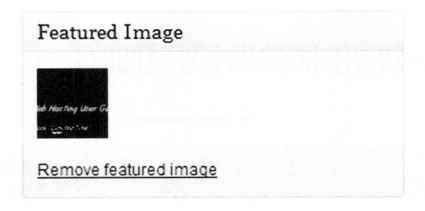

Depending on your theme, your *Featured Image* option might be located somewhere else on the page. The image you upload will be the main picture for your blog article. Take a look at the image below to see what a "Featured Image" could look like on your blog.

A lot of people use Google Images to find a featured image for their articles. Technically you shouldn't do that because a lot of those images are copyrighted. I highly doubt that you'll run into any problems with copyright infringement, but if you want to be 100% professional, you can purchase images from:

1. www.istockphoto.com
2. www.gettyimages.com
3. Type "free royalty free images" into Google to find websites that'll allow you to use free images on your blog. Most of these websites just require that you post a **link** pointing back to their website.

You can also go to www.flickr.com and ask photographers if you can use their images. 95% of Flickr users will say "Yes" and will only ask that you give them credit for the photo.

Bonus Tips About Images: When you upload images, you'll have the option to insert a caption for the image. You can use the caption section to give someone credit for their photo or insert links.

You'll also notice that you have to option to align the images within your blog post. By default the "None" box is checked. Check the box that says "**Left**" to wrap your text around the image and align the image to the left.

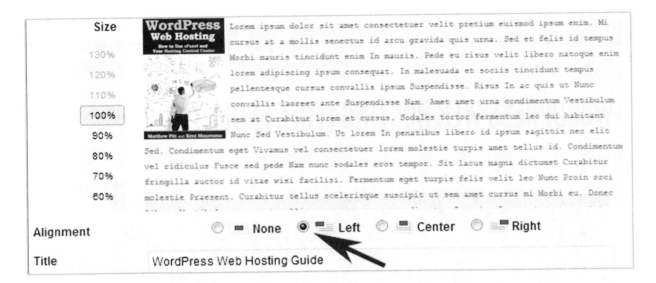

Preview/Publish

On the top right hand corner, you'll see a button that says "**Preview**" and "**Publish.**" Always preview your articles first to make sure they look the way you want them to look.

When you insert an image into your article, the image could drastically change your formatting. You might need to resize the image to make it bigger or smaller by clicking the "**edit**" option on your image.

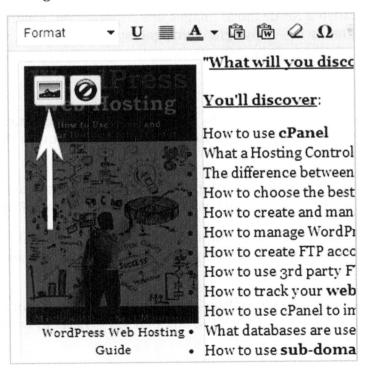

After you proof read your article a few times and you're satisfied with the results, publish the article by clicking the "**Publish**" button on the top right corner.

Bonus Tips: You have the option to "stick" any blog post to the front page. A "**sticky**" post will remain on the front page even when you publish new articles. A "sticky" post will never get pushed to the back.

You'll also notice that you have the option to publish the article immediately; or set WordPress to publish the article at a future date at a specific time. You have to click the "**Edit**" link to expand the list and see these options.

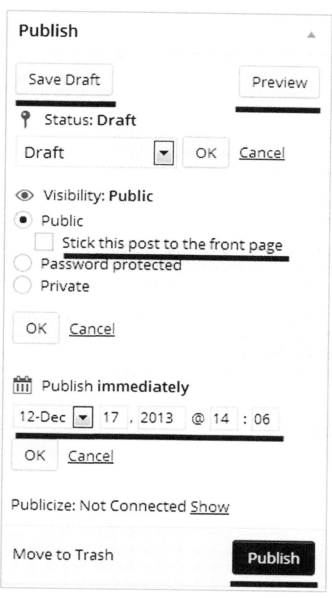

After you've published your article, it's live! Now everybody that visits your website can read your article, share it on Facebook, and leave comments. If you find some spelling errors or you want to make adjustments, just go back to the "**Posts**" tab, click the "Edit" link under the article that you'd like to edit, and make the necessary changes. When you're done, just click the "**Update**" button to publish the updated version.

WARNING: If you decide to update an article, **DO NOT edit the permalink** after you've already published it.

It's called a permalink because it's a **permanent link** to your article. If you edit the permalink after your article has already been published, then search engines like Google will have the wrong link to your article because you've changed it.

If this happens, anybody who clicks on your link through a search engine will get a 404 error that says "*This page doesn't exist.*"

Bonus Tip: I realize that some of you reading this book might already have a WordPress website up and running. If you've changed your permalink settings (per our instructions earlier in this book), then you're going to get 404 errors from search engines too.

If you've changed your permalinks structure in the settings area, then **ALL** your previously published permalinks for all your articles and posts will change. To fix this, you can install a plugin called **Permalink Finder** created by *Keith P. Graham*. Now if someone clicks on your article from Google, this plugin will find the new permalink associated with the article to avoid 404 errors.

Permalink Finder Deactivate Edit	Never get a 404 page not found ag every time. Version 2.3 | By Keith P. Graham |

Chapter 10.

More Dashboard Features: Media Tab

Within your dashboard you'll see a "**Media**" tab. Every time you upload an image into one of your articles, it's automatically saved into the media tab. You can also add images or files **directly** into your media tab if you need to host a file.

Any file that you upload into the "media" tab gets assigned a URL. This is very useful because there are some WordPress widgets that'll request an "Image URL" to display your images.

To find your image URL, click the "**Media**" tab and then click the "**Edit**" link under one of the images that you've uploaded. On the right side of the screen you'll see something that says "File URL." Inside that box you'll see a website address which is the hosted image URL.

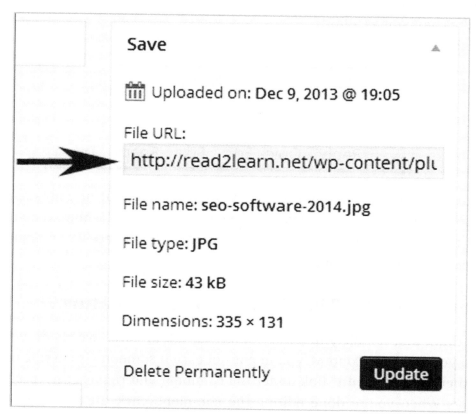

You can copy and paste that link into your web browser, and you'll see that the link will display a webpage only displaying your image.

Keep this in mind if you ever run into a scenario when you're asked for an "Image URL." A lot of people use Photobucket to host their images, but you can use the *media* tab within WordPress because it's more reliable.

Bonus Tip: You can also upload <u>PDF documents</u> into the media tab. This is how people link to PDF documents within their blog posts. Just upload the PDF document, copy the file URL, and link to it within your blog posts or article.

Comments Tab

When someone leaves a comment on your blog, you'll see an alert on your "**Comments**" tab. When you click the "comments" tab, you'll have the option to:

- Approve the comment
- Reply to the comment
- Edit the comment
- Mark the comment as SPAM
- Send the comment to the trashcan

> Submitted on 2013/10/18 at 12:34 pm
>
> thank you man
>
> Unapprove | Reply | Quick Edit | Edit | Spam | Trash

If you want to see how the comment feature works, then log out of your dashboard and leave a comment on one of your articles. Now log back into your dashboard and you'll see a comment alert that shows that you have one comment. You'll receive an <u>email</u> too when someone leaves a comment on your website.

When Should You Use The *"Edit "* Comment Feature?

Some people think that it's okay to leave comments full of curse words on your website. Depending on your website content, you might not care if someone is cursing or not. But if you do care, then click the "**edit**" link under the comment and replace the curse word with something else. When you're done editing the comment, click the "**Update**" button and make sure the "**Approved**" option is checked.

2nd Reason: Your website visitors are prompted to enter their *Website Address* (optional) when leaving a comment, but some people think it's a requirement. If they don't have a website, they might enter something like "www.i-dont-have-a-website.com." You need to delete those types of links because they don't lead anywhere.

When someone leaves a comment and fills in the website option; that'll turn their name into a clickable **outgoing link** on your website. Search engines like Google will scan your website for outgoing links. If you have a lot of outgoing links that don't lead anywhere, then that's bad for search engine optimization.

How To Get Blog Comments

Most internet users have A.D.D. (attention deficit disorder.) They're Twitter tweeting, Facebooking, playing with their iPhone, watching YouTube, and watching Netflix all at the same time.

The reason I bring this up is because **a lot** of people get discouraged when their blog doesn't get a lot of comments when they're first starting out. Don't worry about it! People are so busy doing 10 different things at once that they don't take the time to comment even if they love your article.

You can increase your chance of receiving comments on your website by:

- Asking a question at the end of your article to encourage user interaction.
- Tell people to leave comments! *Some* people need to be told what to do.
- Most importantly, NEVER leave your comments empty! If no one leaves a comment on your articles, then ask your friends and family to leave comments for you. If they don't leave any comments, then add comments in there yourself.

If your website doesn't have any comments, then it'll appear to be a dead website. If your website looks dead, then no one is going to leave a comment. It's a vicious cycle.

If your website already has a couple comments on an article, then someone else might come along, read the existing comments, and add in their 2 cents. It's the bandwagon effect.

Don't worry about other popular websites or blogs that have 30, 40 or even 100 comments. 95% of those comments are **not** genuine. Most people leave comments on "popular" websites just to get a link back to their own website.

If you recall earlier, I mentioned that your name shows up as a **clickable** link that points back to your website when you leave a comment. That's why people leave a ton of comments on popular blogs that get a lot of traffic. They're hoping that a lot of people will click the link from their comment and visit their website too.

That's exactly why you see a lot of comments that only say, *"Great post!"* That's an absolutely useless comment to leave on someone's blog, and now you know why people do it.

Tools Tab

Within your dashboard, you'll see a tab that says "Tools." You can use the tools tab to import and export data. If you recall earlier, I mentioned that some premium WordPress themes come with demo content.

To upload the demo content, you have to use the *Tools* tab and then click on the **WordPress Importer** option. I don't want to go into too much detail about this because the process can be different for your theme.

If you ever need to use the tools tab to import demo content, then your theme will come with instructions showing you exactly how to do it!

Now let's talk about **RSS Feeds**. Do you know what an RSS Feed is?

Chapter 11.

What's an RSS Feed?

An RSS feed is a way for people to subscribe to your websites content. "Feeds" allow users to access your blog content from multiple feed reading services. You've seen the RSS Feed symbol before on other people's websites.

With an RSS Feed, users don't have to visit your website to read your content. Instead, users can access your latest articles directly from their email or portable "Feed Reader" devices.

Learn How RSS Feeds Work

The only way to learn how an *RSS Feed* work is to sign up for one. Google used to have a "feed reader" called Google Reader, but they discontinued the service. Alternatively, you can see how RSS feeds work by using this website: www.cloud.feedly.com. Click the "Get Started" button, and then you'll arrive at a page where you can enter a website URL.

Enter my website (read2learn.net) into the search box, and they'll display a list of websites matching your search. You should only see my website there, so click on it. After you click on my website, you'll see a snippet of my most recent articles along with an image from the article. At the top of the page you'll see a link that says "add to my feedly." If you were to add my website to your "feedly" then you can keep up to date with my latest articles without actually visiting my website.

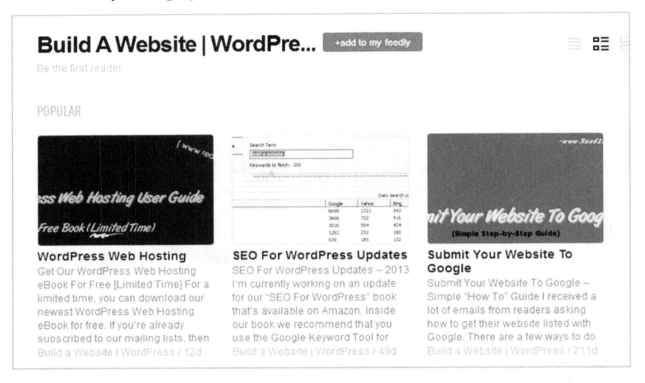

People use feed reader services to save time. Instead of visiting 50 different websites per day to keep up with the latest articles, people will use feed reader services. Feed readers like www.cloud.feedly.com will allow you read articles from multiple websites in one place.

There are other feed reader services that'll allow you to subscribe by clicking the "RSS" icon on the desired website.

After you click the RSS icon, you'll be taken to a page that has a list of my latest articles along with "**Subscribe Now**" buttons. Below the subscribe buttons, you'll see a drop-down list of other available readers that you can use to subscribe. You'll also have the option to subscribe by email. If you were to select the email option, then you'd receive an update by email every time I publish a new article.

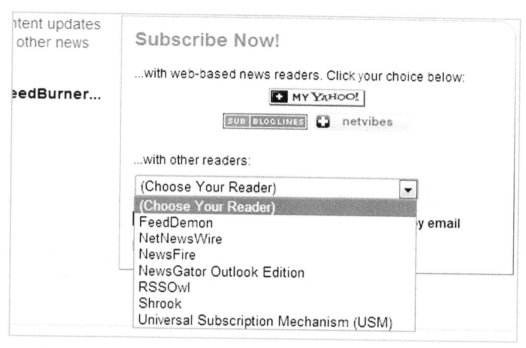

If you'd like to give people the opportunity to subscribe to your website via feed reader services; then you're going to have to add an RSS feed to your website first.

How to Add an RSS Feed To Your Website

Go to www.feedburner.com and enter in your Google username and password. After you sign in, you'll be taken to a page that'll ask you to type in your blog address. Simply type in your website address and hit the "**Next**" button.

On the next screen, you'll see the words *Feed Title* and you'll see your "Feed Address." You can change the *Feed Title* to match the name of your website, and then click the next button!

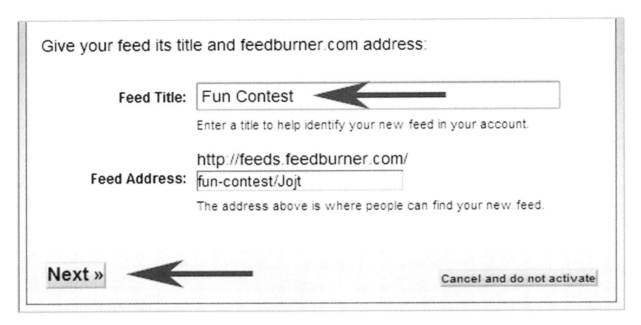

The next screen will say "Congrats!" and display your complete **FeedBurner URL**. You should copy and paste this URL and **save it to a notepad** because you might need this later.

Click the "**Next**" button to arrive at the next screen. On this page you'll need to scroll down and click the check box next to the words, "*I want more! Have FeedBurner Stats also track:*" and press the "Next" button.

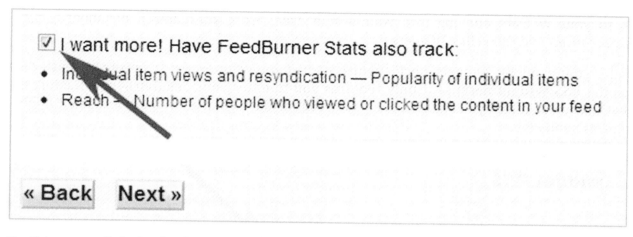

On this page click the "**Publicize**" tab at the top, and then click "**Chicklet Chooser**" on the left column. By default, FeedBurner has already selected the orange colored RSS Feed icon for you. Scroll down the page and you'll see some HTML code that you can paste into a "**Text**" widget on your website.

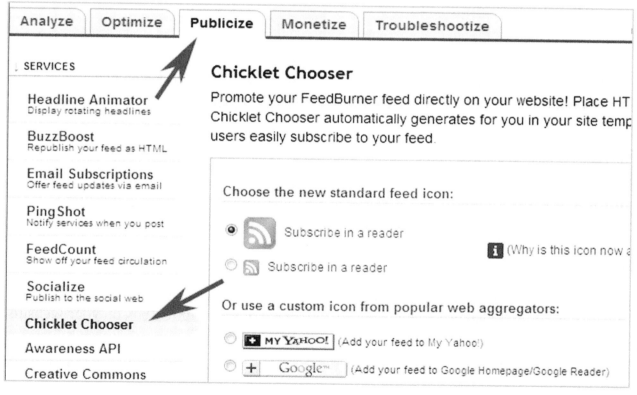

At this point, you have 2 options available:

1. Copy and Paste the HTML code into a <u>"Text" widget</u> on your website
2. Enter your new Feed URL into a <u>"RSS" widget</u>.

Go to your website and log into your admin area. From your admin dashboard, click *Appearances*, and then click *Widgets.*

Under your available widgets, decide which widget you want to use. It's probably easier to use the **RSS Widget** because it only requires you to enter your Feedburner URL address. That's why I said that you should save your Feedburner URL in a notepad because it might come in handy later.

Almost ALL themes will come with some type of RSS widget. If your theme doesn't have an RSS widget, then you have to copy and paste the HTML code from Feedburner into a "**text**" widget.

Now go to your websites homepage to check out your RSS feed! Click it to make sure it works. If it works, then you're ready to go!

TIP: If you haven't written any blog posts on your website, then your RSS Feed won't display any articles.

Bonus Tip

Some internet users have no idea what an RSS Feed is or how to subscribe to it. So as an alternative, you can also use Feedburner to add an email subscription box on your website too.

To add an email subscription box to your website, go back to Feedburner.com and follow these steps:

1. Click the **publicize** tab at the top of the page, and click **Email Subscriptions** on the left column.
2. Click the button at the bottom of the page that says "Activate"

Email Subscriptions

Give your biggest fans another way to keep up with your blog or podcast feed by placing an email subscription form on your site.

After you activate this service, FeedBurner will provide HTML code for a subscription form you should copy and place on your own site.

Note: Email Subscriptions requires that your FeedBurner account uses a valid email address. Visit My Account to double-check your settings.

FeedBurner Email Preview

View a sample message in HTML or Plain Text

How do I know which email format my subscribers will see?

Activate This service is **inactive**

Next, you'll be taken to a page that has some new HTML code. You need to copy and paste that code into a "**Text**" widget on your website. Now your internet readers will have 2 ways to subscribe to your websites content. They can click on your *RSS* button or alternatively enter their email into your Feedburner subscription box.

If they enter their email into your Feedburner subscription box, they'll receive an email every time you write a new blog post on your website.

Bonus Info

In the next chapter, I'll give you a couple resources to help you sell products online.

I'll recommend:

- Shopping Carts that you can easily integrate with your website to sell products.
- Website themes/plugins to create squeeze pages to capture email addresses.
- Email auto responder software.
- How to turn your website into a paid membership site.
- How to easily sell physical products.

Chapter 12.

Do you want to sell products online?

In this short chapter, I will give you a few different websites and other resources to help you sell products and services online.

Email List

You need to build an email list! Every online business has some sort of mailing list. You can use your email list to send out website updates, advertise new products or services, and send out newsletters.

The best auto responder software is provided by "Aweber." The reason I like Aweber is because the customer service is amazing, and their website is easy to use. You can try Aweber for the first 30 days for only $1.

You can visit their website at: www.aweber.com

Squeeze Pages and Sales Pages

A "squeeze page" is a page that is specifically designed to capture a visitor's **first name** and **email address**.

Squeeze pages are important because they help you build your email list fast! I believe the best WordPress theme to create squeeze pages is provided by "Optimize Press." You can visits there website at: www.optimizepress.com

This WordPress theme cost about $97, but it's worth every penny. The training provided to you in the membership area is worth ten times the cost of the product. You can also use OptimizePress to create amazing sells pages, blogs, and membership areas.

OptimizePress works with the Aweber too, so it's perfect. Look at the image below to see an example of a squeeze page I created with OptimizePress.

Shopping Carts

If you want to sell products online and you need a payment processor, you can use **PayPal Business.** With PayPal business, you can accept credit card payments directly on your website.

You can also copy some simple HTML code provided by PayPal and enter that code on your website to create "Buy Now" buttons. When your customers click the "Buy Now" button, they'll be forwarded to PayPal's secure website to complete the purchase.

For more details, visit the website at: www.paypal.com/webapps/mpp/merchant

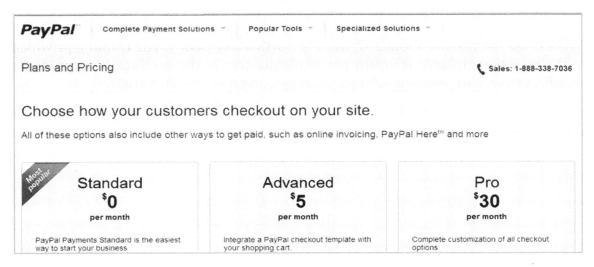

If you're selling digital products like eBooks and MP3's, then you can use "**E-junkie**" to automate the process for you. E-junkie provides a <u>shopping cart</u> and <u>buy now buttons</u> that'll allow you sell downloads and tangible goods on your website.

If you're selling downloads, E-junkie will automate and secure the digital delivery of files and codes. If you are selling tangible goods, E-junkie will automate the shipping calculation and inventory management.

For more details, visit the website at: <u>www.e-junkie.com</u>

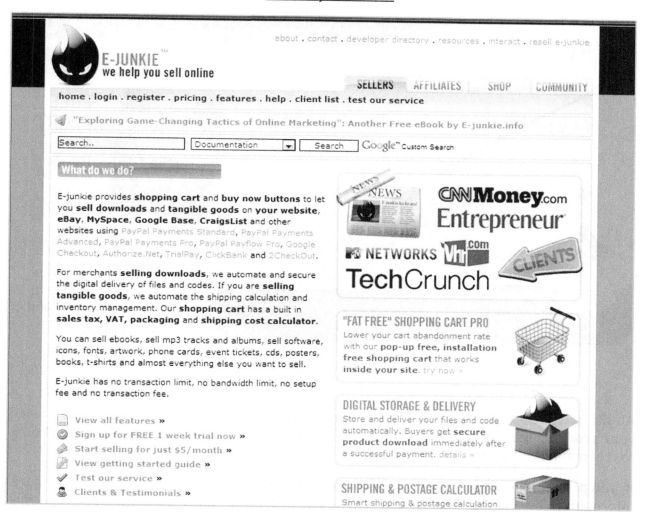

Sell Physical Products

If you want to turn your digital products into physical products, it's a lot easier than you think. You don't have to stock pile physical products.

If you're selling CD's or DVD's, there are companies that will create your CD's or DVD's on demand when someone orders it. Visit these websites for more information:

- www.kunaki.com
- www.disk.com
- www.trepstar.com

If you have a Book/CD combo, you can use a site like Vervante. They actually print CD's, DVD's and Books on demand. You can visit their website at: www.vervante.com

All these websites integrate with PayPal and other shopping carts. So if someone orders your product, your shopping cart will alert the *"Print on demand"* company of your choice to create the product and ship it out.

If you'd also like to sell your physical products on **Amazon**, then you can get more information by visiting this page: www.amazon.com/gp/seller-account/mm-summary-page.html

Create a Membership Site

If you want to create a membership site and collect monthly fees from customers, then you'll need a plugin or script for that.

Here are 2 different sources that you can start with:

- www.member.wishlistproducts.com ($97 non-recurring)
- www.s2member.com (**Free** & Paid Options Starting at $69 non-recurring)

If you decide to go with the FREE option, don't expect to get amazing customer support if any at all. I use the **Free** s2Member plugin for one of my websites, and trust me when I say it's very techincal. I almost paid the $69 just to get customer support, but I finally figured it out a week later.

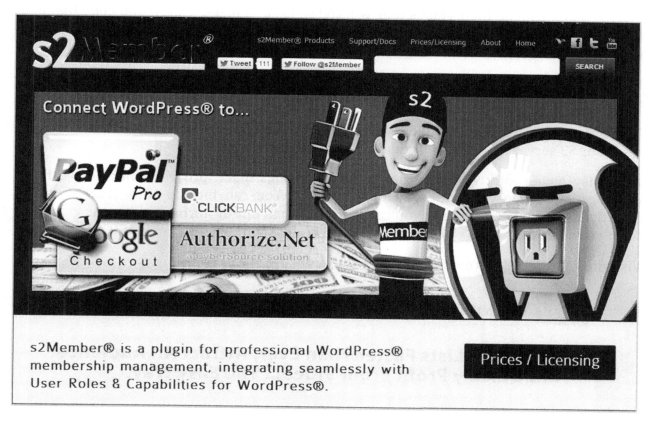

All these membership plugins will integrate with **PayPal** and other popular shopping carts. These membership plugins and scripts also work perfectly with WordPress. Feel free to do your own research as well, but these are a few good resources for you.

Create Video's For Your Website

If you want to use professional videos on your website, then I do NOT recommend using YouTube. A lot of people host all their marketing and business videos on YouTube, and then embed the video on their website. That's a really bad idea.

If you host marketing or <u>overly promotional</u> videos on YouTube, then YouTube reserves the right to delete all your videos and your YouTube account. Creating marketing videos on YouTube goes against their Terms of Service.

YouTube is really designed for people to upload silly videos of themselves or other cool creative short videos, and that's why it's free. You're not supposed to use YouTube to try to sell anything.

Some people get away with it for years, and then suddenly their YouTube account is deleted along with all their videos they worked so hard to make. I know someone that had his YouTube videos up for 3 years! He had over 100 videos and YouTube deleted **all of them.**

Hosting your marketing videos on YouTube is like hosting your website on *Live Journal*. It's not professional and you're not in control.

I recommend using **Easy Video Player**! This video player will host your videos on Amazons S3 server for fast videos that'll never freeze like YouTube.

Also, they have some really amazing security settings that'll prevent other people from copying/embedding your video on their website. You can include "**Buy Now**" buttons directly inside your videos, and you can include "email opt-in" forms inside your videos to build your email list. This video player also integrates with Aweber, so it's 100% business!

Visit the website for more information: <u>www.easyvideoplayer.com</u>

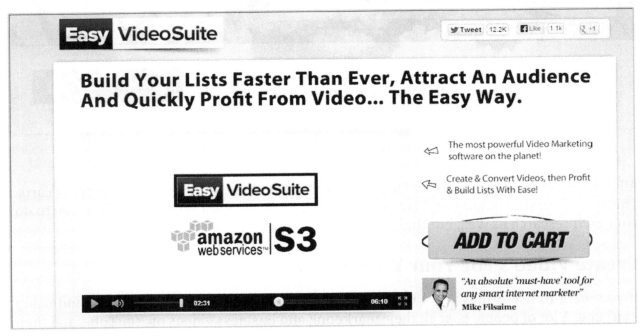

If you want to create amazing **video slide shows**, I recommend using *Animoto*. You can use this service for free, but you're limited to what you can do. I have the pro version because you can create longer slide shows and produce videos in High Definition. The website is: www.animoto.com

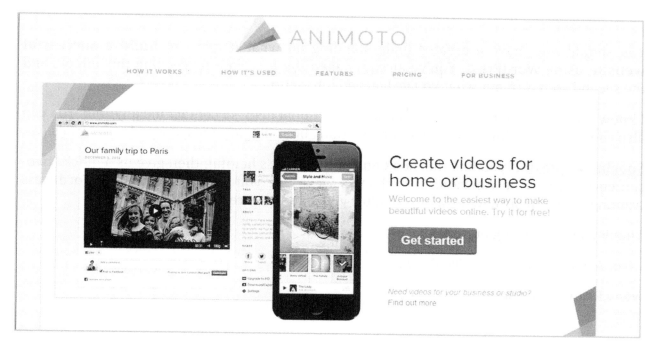

Conclusion

You should now have a greater understanding on what it takes to **build a successful website** using WordPress. You've already taken the first step by reading this eBook, and the second step is to put what you've learned into action.

I know you'll still have questions and need additional help, so contact me anytime. You can also check out our blog for updated information about plugins and a few video tutorials.

Special Request: If you like this book and you think it's helpful; then give us a quick "two-sentence" review on Amazon! In exchange, we'll give you free access to our WordPress training videos. Just send me an email after you leave your review.

Thank you for reading our book!

-*Kent Mauresmo & Anastasiya Petrova*

www.Read2Learn.net

PDF Version of This eBook

To download the PDF version of this book, visit the link below:

www.read2learn.net/2013-edition

More From This Author

*"WordPress Web Hosting:
How to Use cPanel and Your Hosting Control Center"*

*"SEO For WordPress:
Discover How To Easily Get Your Website on Page #1 of Google"*

"Book Publishing Blueprint:
How To Self Publish & Market Your Books...Fast!"

CPSIA information can be obtained at www.ICGtesting.com.
Printed in the USA
LVOW02s0203080314

376557LV00001B/5/P